Life Unarmed

My Story

Diana L. Taylor

ISBN 978-1-64349-174-5 (paperback)
ISBN 978-1-64349-175-2 (digital)

Christian Faith Publishing, Inc.
832 Park Avenue
Meadville, PA 16335
www.christianfaithpublishing.com

Printed in the United States of America

Acknowledgments

I would like to dedicate this book to God, my heavenly Father. Without whom, I wouldn't even be here, and this book would never have happened; and thru whom I found forgiveness for all those I felt had hurt and wronged me in my life. Thank you, Father.

I want to give a huge thank-you to my mom and dad for all they did for me and taught me. Love and miss you both.

I would also like to acknowledge my dad's wife, Betty. It's been a long, and at times an ugly road between us. I know and believe that God has healed all the ugly wounds between you and I, and we are a better people today because of all the trials we've gone through. I love you!

I want to say thank you to my uncle Tom and aunt Betty for being like a second mom and dad to me. I love and miss you both.

Next, I want to thank my grandma and granddad Rye for all they taught me also. Love and miss you both too.

Last but not least, I want to thank Sister Ida, who looked after me whenever I was in the hospital. She helped me learn to read, helped me with schoolwork, and was a great friend to me. She could get thru to me when no one else could. Thank you all.

I, Diana Lynn Cooper, came into this world on March 13, 1957, at 12:09 a.m. to Herbert D. and Frances B. Cooper at the Susan B. Allen Memorial Hospital in the city of El Dorado, Kansas. My parents were very happy and proud. I was their firstborn child. Two years later, in September of 1959, my brother Robin Dean (Rob) was born. My parents again were very proud and happy. We lived like any typical family. My dad worked for Beech Aircraft Company. My mom stayed at home and took care of the home and my brother and me. We eventually moved to Wichita, Kansas, so Dad would be closer to work and the drive wouldn't be so far for him. We lived in a little gray house on a street called Ash next to a drainage canal. It was July 6, 1961, and I was four years old. Dad was at work, and at about 11:40 a.m., I was outside playing at a neighbor's house, and I climbed an electrical pole that was in their backyard. I climbed about thirty to forty feet up when I came into contact with the overhead lines and was electrocuted. Over seven thousand volts of electricity went through my body at that moment. The force of the electrical shock then blew me off the pole. I fell the thirty to forty feet to the ground. The power dimmed in the entire neighborhood as I lay there on the ground burning. An ambulance was called, and I was taken to St. Joseph Hospital there in Wichita.

The doctors said that the electrical shock I took actually stopped my heart from beating. The force of the shock that blew me off the pole actually saved my life, because I hit the ground with such force that it jolted my heart into beating again. The doctors gave me a very slim chance of survival. I had received third-degree burns to over 60 percent of my body. Doctors said that they would treat my wounds and keep me comfortable but told my parents to prepare for a probable funeral; but if I survived 7 days, they would do everything they could to help me survive. My parents refused to accept my impending death. So everyone waited on pins and needles, but survive I did. My right arm was burned almost completely off. Doctors said my arm had to be amputated just below the shoulder. Dad wanted to see why, because my arm had been wrapped up in bandages. When they removed the bandages, all that was there was bone. No skin or flesh or meat. Dad said he got real queasy and lightheaded when he saw my arm or lack thereof. He then understood the reason for the amputation. Sometime later, gangrene set into my right leg, and the doctors said it had to be amputated also. Dad said that he feared the doctors would remove more than what they told *him*, and he wanted to see exactly where they were going to amputate my leg. The doctors removed my right leg, from just below the knee.

Only by the grace of God did I survive all this. Doctors said that I am a walking, talking miracle. I went through many months of skin grafts and surgeries while in the hospital. I remember being wrapped up like a mummy in bandages and gauze. My burns were so severe that they would ooze. The nurses couldn't just pull off the bandages for changing, so they would take me down to a special room with a huge whirlpool tub. The tub was so huge to a small child and full of swirling water. I was absolutely terrified of it. The nurses would put me into a type of swing and slowly lower me into the water to loosen and remove the bandages from my skin. I would scream at them to stop. I begged them not to put me in there, but they won't listen to me. I was terrified of drowning.

This was done to me many times over the next many weeks. When electricity enters a body, it must also exit. In my case, it exited out my back. My back was blown full of holes. Many skin grafts had to be performed to cover my back. Skin was removed from my left leg and thigh and also from the remainder of my right thigh, and also from my left arm. It was all placed onto my back. My face was spared from any burns and scarring. I do have a scar on the right side of my neck, one on my arm near the elbow, and one on the back of my arm. Most of my back is scarred, down to, and including my right hip. My left ear was burnt to the extent that the skin chipped, making the top of my ear pointed, like Mr. Spock in the movie series *Star Trek*. There were a lot of nuns who worked in the hospital where I was. They were called "sisters," and they wore their habits. One in particular who helped take care of me was called Sister Ida. I will never forget her. She could get through to me and get me to do things that no one else could do. She was a wonderful lady. I even have a picture of her and me with a Chatty Cathy doll that she had given to me while in the hospital. She came to see me every day. I looked forward to her visits. If I had been good and had done what I was asked to do by the nurses, then she would take me down to the playroom to play awhile. That was always the highlight of my day. We would play with the toys and put puzzles together, or she would just read some of the storybooks to me. Back in my room, I had tons of get-well cards from everywhere and everyone, and my mom and Sister Ida would read them to me. Sister Ida was like a second mom to me, except that she was a nun and wore a habit. I loved her very much. After my wounds and amputations healed, a cast was made of my stump in order to build me an artificial leg. Before I got my first leg, my means of getting around was in a wheelchair or crawling on my knees or hopping on my one leg. When my artificial leg was completed, I literally had to learn to walk all over again. I hated that leg. It hurt me. It was a foreign object on my body. I remember falling down, constantly. I didn't want to wear it. I was taken to physical therapy to learn how to walk with it. I continued to complain but to no avail. My parents and therapists pushed and encouraged me to learn to wear it and walk with it. In time, I did learn, and the leg became like a part of me. I now have two legs, not just one. The doctors told my parents that the worst thing they could do was to treat me like an invalid. Doctors said to "just let her be a kid and do what other kids do—that in time I would learn my limitations." I don't think I ever learned them, limitations, that is. I didn't see myself as different from anyone else, maybe because I was still too young yet. I could run, climb trees, and even learned to ride a bike. The phrase that I heard most often growing up was, "Figure it out." Mom and Dad were not going to do things for me, and that if I wanted to do something, I had to "figure it out" for myself. For instance, tying my shoes. Mom said she could not keep tying my shoes for me forever, so I had to learn to do it for myself. I started by using my one hand and my mouth. I did get them tied and got really good at it.

Then came school. In the beginning, grade school was very hard for me. I would come home from school every day crying. The other kids would laugh at me and make fun of me and call me names. Names like retardo, gimp, and crip, short for crippled. They wouldn't play with me, because I looked different physically from them. Mom tried to comfort me. She would tell me to ignore them, that after a while they would leave me alone which I learned later is not true. The parents of some of the kids would not allow their kids to play with me. They thought that I had cancer or something like it. Back then, not much was known about cancer. Thoughts were that maybe you could get it through touch, so instead of inquiring as to what had actually happened to me, they assumed that I must have cancer and that if their kids were to be around me, they might get it also. The parents feared that their kids' limbs would fall off too. I was just too young to understand why no one would play with me. Peoples' ignorance was the worst. They would assume instead of inquire. Some of the kids would make things up about me. They would see the scars on me and assume that I had been in a house fire or a car crash that burned. Those stories always went around. The street that I lived on had two families with girls my age whom I played with. One girl was Cindy; the other girl was Nancy. We played together almost daily. Cindy's family allowed me to come into their home and play, and on occasion, I got to spend the night with Cindy. Nancy's family never allowed me into their home, ever. I could only play with Nancy on their porch. She wasn't allowed to come to my home either. I never knew why, just accepted it.

At school, there were two games that I could play very well on the playground at recess. One was kickball. I could kick the ball really hard with my artificial leg. I just wasn't a very fast runner. The other game was tetherball. I could really hit the ball hard with my fist and knock it around the pole. My opponent would have a hard time hitting it back. I also learned how to roller-skate. I really like skating. My parents would take me to the local roller rink almost every weekend. I loved it and was a pretty good skater. The wooden leg (as I called it) that I wore as a kid had to be strapped on. Once when I was at the skating rink, I had fallen down. When I did the strap on, my leg broke. When that happened, my leg came off and went down the rink upright on the skate. It was very embarrassing but really kind of funny. I had to ask someone to go and get my leg and bring it back to me. That doesn't happen very often in one's life. In school, my favorite subject was spelling. I was pretty good at it. I participated in spelling bees at school. I really enjoyed them. Over time, grade school got easier for me because the kids got used to me. There were always those few kids who never eased up on me. Most of the games played on the playground at school were team games. The teams were chosen by team captains, which I never got to be. I was always the last one chosen. No one wanted me on their team. Whenever we couldn't play outside due to weather conditions, we had our recesses in the classrooms. One particular game that was played was the thumb game. Two or three kids were chosen and went to the front of the class. The rest of us had to put our heads down and close our eyes and raise our thumbs up. No peeking was allowed. The two or three chosen kids would move around the classroom quietly and touch the thumbs of various kids.

When your thumb got touched, you put it down. After a few minutes, the teacher would tell us to raise our heads. We then had to guess who touched our thumbs. In all the years that I participated in that game, my thumb was never touched. All schools have bullies, and my school was no exception. I was threatened constantly of being beat up—mostly by older kids. Luckily, I never was, but the fear was always there. I have three brothers, but they can't defend me, because they are all younger than I. The only protection I have is from God, and he did protect me. I was a Scout. First, I was a Brownie Scout. When I got a little older, I became a Girl Scout. We had to sell cookies and calendars to raise money for Scout camp. A lot of people would not buy from me. I could never understand why. My family, grandparents, aunts, and uncles and so on could only buy so many to help me out.

The only way that I could attend camp was that my parents would have to make up the difference. I was unaware of this until years later. Dad taught my brothers and me how to swim. I also took lessons at the YWCA when I was a Brownie Scout. I earned a certificate for that. When I first started going to our local swimming pool, the lifeguards would watch me like a hawk. They feared that I would drown. After they realized that I could swim and, at the very least, dog paddle, they didn't watch me so closely. Even though I only had one arm and a wooden leg, I could actually swim in a straight line. Most people expected me to swim in a circle. Well I didn't, to most peoples' amazement. Another game that I was good at was called jacks.

The game consisted of small metal pointed jacks and a small rubber ball. I could play that game very well. My hand was large, so I was able to pick up and hold several jacks at once. I won ribbons at summer camp for playing jacks.

Summers were great for my brother Robin and me. We got to spend two to three weeks on our aunt Betty and uncle Tom's farm. We are city kids going to the farm. The farm was like an amusement park to us. We loved it. Aunt Betty is our moms' sister, and Uncle Tom is our dads' brother. Yes, brothers married sisters. We have other aunts and uncles whom we love, but Aunt Betty and Uncle Tom are our favorites. They also have four kids, our cousins. They are Mike, Pam, Debbie, and little Tom. I guess that makes us eight kids' double cousins, but none of us look alike. We get up and help with the chores just like our cousins do. We have helped milk the cows and gather the eggs. We also helped in the garden. We also got to drive the tractor and help in the fields. Swimming in the pond was far different from swimming in our local pool. The farm didn't have a bathroom. It did, however, have an outhouse. That sure was different from what we were used to, but it was cool. At night, we took baths in a galvanized tub with water heated on the cookstove. We all went to church on Sunday morning. The church was a country church. Both my parents and aunt and uncle grew up in this church. There isn't any better church in the world than an old country church. The church didn't have a bathroom either. It also had an outhouse. Back at the farm, there was plenty of time for play. My favorite thing to do was climbing trees. Most of the time, I got stuck up in the trees.

Aunt Betty had to come and get me down. She got so mad at me and told me to stay down out of the trees. As soon as I could, I was right back up in the trees again. Although we probably weren't supposed to, we chased the cows in the field. My grandma and my granddad (my moms' parents) are the greatest people. We love them so very much and loved to go to their house. They lived in a town a few miles from our aunt and uncles' farm. Grandma was kind, gentle, and very loving, but very firm. She would make you go out and get a switch off the tree for spanking you with, and it had better be a good one. Grandma was always humming or singing gospel songs all day, every day. Aunt Betty did the same thing. Their homes were always full of singing and humming. Grandma was always surrounded by grandkids and babies. Granddad worked for the railroad. Grandma took care of the house and the kids and tended to the garden. They were very much God-fearing people. My family, mom, dad, brothers, and I got to go visit the grandparents and the aunts and uncles a few times each year. We couldn't wait to get there and didn't want to leave when we had to go home. Our family including extended family is a very close family. Back home in Wichita, when I was about eight years old, a young couple moved into the house right next door to ours. Their names were Bill and Betty. She was pregnant with their first child. The child born was a girl named Kim. My parents and Bill and Betty became good and fast friends. A couple of years later, Betty gave birth to their second child, a boy named Steven. When Steven was a few months old and Kim was between two and three years, I was allowed to watch them from time to time. They became my first babysitting job. The kids would already be down for the night when I would arrive to sit for them. I was paid fifty cents an hour, and my mom was nearby if I needed help, which I never did.

On the streets around our school, we had crossing guards. They were the sixth graders, and they would hold out these large Stop signs to stop traffic so kids could cross the streets safely. They were there before and after school. Only kids in sixth grade were allowed to be crossing guards. Naturally, I wanted to be one when I got to the sixth grade. The school officials said that I couldn't do it, because I wouldn't be able to hold the Stop sign with only one arm. My parents talked to the school and got them to give me a chance to try. They agreed but put another person with me to take over in case I couldn't do it. Well, I was able to do it, and do it very well, and without any help, thank you very much. I received a certificate at the end of the year for being a crossing guard. I still have the certificate to this day.

My seventh-grade year in junior high school was awful. I went from a small grade school to a large junior/senior high school mixed. I didn't know many kids. I was really bullied and made fun of at this school. I lived under a daily threat of being beat up. I was raised so very sheltered and naïve. The only place that I was truly comfortable was at home or at church. We went to church every Sunday morning and Sunday night, and Wednesday night Bible study. The other kids in the church did not tease me or make fun of me. I was accepted by and comfortable around them and other church members also. I really don't remember much about my seventh-grade year in junior high school. I just tried to keep to myself. My parents decided to move and get me out of that school, so they decided to have a house built across town. We moved the summer before I started eighth grade. My third and youngest brother, David, was about a year old. My three brothers are Robin Dean, Joseph Lee (Joe), and David Wayne. Dad and Mom both worked, so I got to take care of my brothers that summer. My parents said that I would get paid ten dollars a week to care for my brothers. My brother Robin then threw a fit, because he felt that he was too old to be looked after. He felt that since he was almost twelve years old and helped with Joe and David that he should get paid also. The folks agreed with him and decided to split the ten dollars between us and gave each of us five dollars. It was I who then threw a fit but to no avail. Robin and I fought about that all summer. I didn't feel like he was doing enough to get any money. In fact, he didn't do anything to help with the boys. The only thing he did was give me a hard time. Robin and I were always fighting about something. I was older and made sure he always knew it, but he was physically stronger and made sure that I knew it. One time, we got into this huge fight. I don't remember why, but I went to my room and got one of my old legs that I could no longer wear, took it, and swung it at his head. I hit him right in the temple with the knee part of the leg. He dropped like a rock to the floor and didn't move. At first, I thought he was just faking, so I shook him. He didn't move, so I gently kicked at him, but there was still no movement, so after a few minutes, I realized that he was really out cold. I thought that I had killed him. *Oh my God, my dad is going to beat my ass for killing my brother*, I thought. I was really scared, but then I got down and listened to his chest and heard his heart beating and knew that he was still alive. Oh, thank God for that. I knew that when Robin woke up, I better not be around. I knew that he would do more than just knock me out for what I had done to him. I was right. When he woke up, he tried to get at me. I had locked the boys and myself in the bathroom. I had everything that I would need for them. That was where I stayed until my folks got home. I did get into trouble with the folks for what I did and was told never to use my leg as a weapon again on my brothers. Yeah, right. I remember one time when my brother Joe was acting up. I got really angry at him, so I put him in the clothes dryer and turned it on. He went around one time, and I let him out. He never acted up again like that, because I would threaten to put him back in the dryer. Dad had this really old pickup truck in the garage. I remember that it had a button you had to push to start it. It was also a stick shift on the floor. Brother Robin would get into it and pretend to drive. One day, Robin and I were playing around inside the truck. Of course, we were not supposed to be in or even around the truck, but like most kids, we didn't do as we were told. My parents weren't there; I thought they would never know. Somehow, the truck got put into reverse, and we didn't know it. I was horsing around and pushed the Start button. The engine started, and the truck went through the garage door. So much for what the parents would never know. We knew that we were in deep trouble. When Dad came home from work, Robin and I blamed each other for what had happened. We both got into a lot of trouble and were grounded for a really long time. Needless to say, Dad had to replace the garage door, and we never did that again. Robin and I fought all the time, and I mean physical fighting. Dad got so tired of us fighting that he took the garden hose and made a circle out of it in the yard and made Robin and I get into the middle of it. He said that we had to fight it out inside the ring. I complained that it wouldn't be a fair fight, because Robin had two hands to my one. So Dad made Robin put one arm behind his back in his pants. He had to fight me with only one arm to make us even. When we were told to fight, then, of course, we didn't want to. Dad would then say that we had to kiss on the lips and tell each other that we loved the other and make up. We hated that and didn't want to do it, but Dad made us. I think that Dad's reasoning was, maybe we wouldn't fight so much if we had to do the making-up part that we hated so much. I guess maybe it worked after a while, because we quit fighting so much or at least we got more careful about not getting caught at it.

On the street where we lived, some of the other kids had mini-bikes (small motorized motorcycles). Dad bought Robin and me one. The throttle was on the right-hand side of the handlebars, making it impossible for me to operate because of only having a left arm. Dad switched the throttle to the left side of the handlebars so I could ride it also. That made Robin really mad because he said that it made our minibike sissified. He hated that. The minibike was yet another thing for us two to fight about, or should I say fight over? I did a lot of babysitting that year round the neighborhood. There was a family down the block who had four kids whom I sat with a lot. I got seventy-five cents an hour to sit for them, and I sat for them weekly. There was an older couple who lived next door to us, and the man's elderly mother lived with them. She was in a wheelchair. I would sit with her so they could go out from time to time. I was paid one dollar an hour to sit with her; boy, was I making money now. The family who lived right across the street from us had six kids. Their oldest, a girl named Ronna, was my age. She and I became real good friends and hung out together. One day, while my mom was at work, I started bleeding. I had started my period for the first time, only I didn't know what was happening to me. I had not been told about this. I thought that I was going to bleed to death. I went to Elva, my friend Ronna's mom, and she explained what was happening to me and then called my mom at work, and she got me took care of.

When my folks came home from work my mom told my dad that I had begun my period, and then my dad came to me to have the "talk." All Dad said to me was, "If you play, you will pay." I somehow knew exactly what he meant. That was the whole lump sum of the sex talk that I got. I knew about sex from school and my friend Ronna. She told me a lot about it because she had experienced it. To me, she was worldly because of that. I was not allowed to have sex until my wedding night. That is what we have been taught at home and in church: you must remain a virgin until you get married.

That year, when Christmas came, Robin and I got into major trouble and almost lost our Christmas. The Christmas tree was up, and there were decorations up and presents under the tree. One evening, while our parents were out, we opened up some of the presents. I opened the ones that had my name on them, and Robin opened his. We discovered that my presents had Robin's name on them, and his presents had my name on them. After we saw what they were, we carefully taped them up and put them back under the tree. No one would ever be the wiser. Well, Christmas Day came, and Robin and I were so excited to open our presents that we weren't thinking and handed each other the opposite presents that we knew were ours.

Mom asked why I had Robin's presents and why Robin had mine. Unless we took a sneak peek, we shouldn't have known that the names were switched. We were so busted. They knew what we had done and threatened to take away all our presents and have no Christmas at all. We cried and begged and did not lose Christmas. We did get big-time grounded, again, but we never did that again.

That winter, I experienced my first and only real-life blizzard, so far, anyway. It snowed and snowed and snowed. The wind blew and blew like I had never seen before. Wichita was literally shut down. The schools were closed for days. Cars were literally buried. I had never seen anything like it before or since. Snow was so high everywhere. It was halfway up people's houses. It was one crazy storm we had. All the snow didn't melt for weeks. Later that spring at school, in gym class, I had a teacher who didn't like me much. We as a class had gone outside onto the field to do relay races. We were divided up into two groups. We were racing against each other, and the teacher had a stopwatch timing us. When I was up next to run, the teacher told me to go and take a seat. When I asked her why, she told me that I couldn't even run fast enough to even get on the clock. I was so embarrassed and angry that I ran into the school to the gym locker room, changed my clothes, and ran home. Now I rode a bus to school because we lived about five miles from school, maybe more. I ran until I couldn't run anymore; then I walked. Naturally, the school contacted my parents. I told them what had happened, and I said I would not return to gym class. They spoke with the school and the gym teacher. I was transferred to another gym class with a different gym teacher. I never got an apology from that teacher, but I didn't have to deal her ever again. There was another girl in the school who had an artificial leg. Everyone liked her. She was very popular, but not me. I thought, *Why am I treated like an outcast? No one likes me. I just want to be like everyone else. I live under a threat of being beat up. Will this last my whole life? Are people going to want to beat me up all my life?* I ended up skipping school frequently. I just hated going to school. My parents both worked so they didn't know that I was not catching the school bus. Then my stump got messed up, and I had to have surgery on it, and, of course, there was even more time out of school. It took quite a while to heal. When all was said and done, I missed so much school that my parents decided to hold me back instead of allowing me to go into the ninth grade. I didn't want to go to school to begin with, and I had to take eighth grade twice. I was furious with my parents. I begged them "not to do this to me. Please let me go on to ninth grade with the rest of my classmates." My dad was adamant. He didn't budge. "You are taking eighth grade again," he said. It would just give the kids even more to tease me about, I argued, but they still didn't listen. I hated my parents. I couldn't believe they were doing it to me. I was still not able to attend school yet because my stump hadn't completely healed yet. My friend Ronna, from across the street, was bringing my schoolwork home for me to do. I was not able to do the work, because it was ninth-grade work. The school did not hold me back like my parents had insisted they do. A few weeks went by before my dad found out. When he did, it hit the fan. He went to the school and raised all kinds of hell and forced the school to put me back into the eighth grade. This time, he got the job done. I was back in the eighth for the second time. When I was finally able to attend school physically, I was embarrassed to be there with what were eighth graders. I felt stupid. I just wanted to die.

Things seemed to be different between my parents. I didn't know exactly why or what it is. They didn't seem to be as happy as they used to be. I saw my mom crying when she thought no one was watching. We were raised to never question our parents or our elders. We were to always trust them and trust authority figures.

We never saw our parents argue or fight, or even had an unkind word toward one another. It just didn't happen. But something wasn't right. I remember one night, in the middle of the night, my youngest brother, David, was crying upstairs in his room. My bedroom was below his downstairs. I listened to him cry for a while and wondered why mom wasn't getting up to take care of him. My parents' room was right next to his. Surely Mom can hear him crying. After some time, I finally got up to go upstairs and see about David, and I saw Mom asleep on the couch in the living room on the main floor. That seemed very strange to me. I went on up and tended to David and got him settled back down to sleep. I myself went back to bed, still wondering why Mom was on the couch. I thought, *Why isn't she in the bedroom with Dad?*

They always slept together in their room. It was very strange to me. The next morning, when I got up, you couldn't tell she had slept on the couch. Dad seemed to be gone a lot. He took off and would be gone for a couple of hours, which he had never done before. Once when he came home from wherever he had been, he was bent down, doing something to the wheel of his truck; and I noticed on the bald spot on top of his head a pair of lip prints in a sort of pink shade of lipstick. I knew it wasn't from my mom. Mom didn't wear much makeup, and it wasn't her shade of lipstick, anyway. I never questioned or said anything to my dad, nor did I say anything to my mom about what I had seen. I don't even know if my mom saw the lip prints or not. I didn't know what to think about what I had seen. I just had to put it out of my mind, and not think about it anymore.

It was sometime after that when on one Saturday morning I was watching a show called *American Bandstand*, hosted by Dick Clark. I watched this show mostly every Saturday morning. This particular Saturday, Dick Clark introduced a singing group called the Osmond Brothers. A fourteen-year-old boy named Donny Osmond was the lead singer. Oh, my goodness gravy, that was it. I was officially an Osmond fan. In reality, I was hooked on Donny Osmond. I was in love with Donny. I had been in love with Elvis Presley up to that point, but he (Elvis) was much older than I. Donny was my age, so I pushed my love for Elvis to the side to make room for Donny Osmond. I just couldn't get enough of him. I began using my babysitting money to buy those teen magazines. I would read every article or interview on or about the Osmond's and Donny. I collected every poster that I could get my hand on. Donny's favorite color was purple, so that became my favorite color. I even had my bedroom painted purple. My new winter coat was purple. I don't know why I even bothered getting my room painted, because I had every inch of wall space and ceiling plastered with posters of the Osmond's and Donny, but mostly Donny. Then one day, I learned that the Osmonds were coming to Wichita, Kansas, to do a concert. *I have to go. No, I must go.* The tickets to go are six dollars. *I can do babysitting, but that won't get me enough money. What can I do to earn more money? I know I can collect pop bottles and turn them in for cash. I can get five cents for every bottle I turn in. Between babysitting and pop bottles, I earned enough money to buy the ticket. All I need now is an outfit to wear, but what?* I talked to my mom, and with the two of us, we created the perfect outfit. Mom was a seamstress, so she was able to make the outfit that I wanted to wear. My best friend from school, her name is Lettie Smith, and I went together to the concert. My dad took us and dropped us off. What a night it was! At one point during the concert when Donny sang "Puppy Love," I saw him pointing directly at me. I just knew he was singing to me. Toward the end of the concert, Lettie and I made our way toward the exit where the Osmonds would be leaving the building. When the concert ended and the Osmonds were exiting, I reached out and actually touched Donny Osmond. Oh, my goodness gravy, that was it. I could just lie down and die of pure joy and happiness. I had touched Donny Osmond, the boy I loved. Of course, I knew that I could never ever wash my hand, not ever again. Then my dad came and picked us up. I told him what had happened, and he thought that I was nuts. He said that I would have to wash my hand sometime. When I got home that night, I put my handprint all over my mirror to preserve the Donny Osmond feel. I thought, *Life just couldn't get any better than this. I just know that, someday, I will grow up and marry Donny Osmond. I am, after all, his biggest and number one fan. Donny and Diana Osmond, it has such a nice ring to it. I can't wait for that magical day. I love him so much, and I know just about everything about him and his family.* But while my life felt like it was riding on a high, my family was falling apart. Sometime after that, my dad moved out of the house.

I remember one day when I was home from school, the doorbell rang. When I answered the door, there was a police officer there. He asked for Frances Cooper (my mom). I called to my mom, and she came to the door. The officer asked if she was Frances Cooper, and when she said yes, he tried to hand her some papers, and she started screaming, "No, no, no!" and refused to take them. He finally just put them in her hand and left. She continued to cry, "No, no, no," and then fell to the floor crying. I sat there on the floor with her and cried also. I didn't even know why she was crying or what the papers were. After a while, she told me that the papers were divorce papers. My dad wanted a divorce from my mom. She said it was because he didn't love her anymore. Mom said that they both love us kids very much and that that won't change. During this time that my family was falling apart, I learned that our family friends the Rosses were also getting divorced. By now they had three children. The third child is a girl named Melissa (Missy), and she was just a baby. I found all this very strange—two close families divorcing at the same time. After a few months, my mom decided to go and live with her parents (my grandparents), 150 miles away. She felt it was best that we kids stay with our dad because we were still in school, beside the fact that she had no way to support us at the time. After my mom left, Betty seemed to always be around. She and my dad were going out a lot. She was at our house at night until late. She wore makeup and lipstick, the same color lipstick that I saw on top of my dad's head months ago. I wondered about them a lot, but again I didn't say a word to anyone. I remember the day my dad came and asked me if I liked Betty. Of course I liked her; I had known her and Bill, her husband, and their kids for years. I had babysat for them. I knew they were good people. I was having a really hard time with this divorce thing. I was only fourteen years old. My mom was not there, and I really needed her. I just didn't understand why it was happening to my family. I never ever saw or heard my folks argue or fight, or even had a harsh word toward one another. Other families that I know that got divorced had always fought and argued loudly and threw things. That just never happened in our home. *Why isn't my dad happy with my mom? Why does he want a divorce? Mom doesn't want one.* From what I understood about divorce, one of the parents moves away, and the kids never see that parent again. I didn't want that. I love both my parents, and so do my brothers. I didn't want to lose either one of them, but what could I have possibly done? Betty tried to step in, and I didn't like it one bit. I just can't say or do anything about it. We were taught that children are to be seen and not heard. We had no voice. The next few weeks for me seemed foggy, like I was walking around in a daze. Eventually, Dad told Robin and me that we had to go before a judge and tell him where we want to live once the divorce is final, with him or with Mom. We were told that wherever Robin and I choose to go, then that is where Joe and David will go also. Robin and I discussed this between ourselves.

Robin said that he wanted to live with Mom, and so did I. That meant that Joe and David will go to Mom's also. Now that left our dad without any of us, no kids at all, and none of us would ever see him again. I began to feel sorry for dad at the thought of making this choice. I just didn't know what to do. Robin said his mind was made up—that he was going to Mom. I wanted to go to Mom's also, and I just didn't know what to. Dad said that he did not want us kids split up. I didn't want to do this at all. I really wanted to live with my mom, but I didn't want to never see my dad again. Then, one day, my dad came to me and said that if I chose him, he would take me to Provo, Utah, where the Osmonds lived, to possibly meet them and see where they lived. Well, that made my decision an easy one. I decided to tell the judge that I would live with my dad.

It was agreed that Robin would live with Mom and probably the younger boys also. At least, this way, Dad would have one of us four kids. Since Robin and I wouldn't be around each other, there wouldn't be any fighting between us. That was a good thing for him and me. The day came for us to go before the judge. Robin and I told the judge our decisions. The judge then ruled that Robin would go and live with Mom, and that I and Joe and David would live with Dad. I thought, *No, that is not what is supposed to happen. I am the only one that is supposed to live with Dad. The boys should all be going to Mom's.* I sure didn't see that coming. I felt guilty, and I felt bad for Mom for losing three of her children, especially David, the baby. I was thinking, *What have I done? This is my fault.* I just knew that my mom would hate me for what I have done. All of this happened because I felt sorry for my dad and the fact that he promised me a trip to Utah to see the Osmonds. Dad had no idea that I wanted to change my mind. I really wanted to live with Mom. I couldn't tell him, though. I love my dad and also fear his stern hand. I just couldn't ever speak the way I really felt about anything. After all, we were to be seen and not heard. Even if we were asked about something, we were also taught that if you can't say anything nice, then don't say anything at all, so our true feelings were never spoken.

Eventually, Dad came to me and told me that he wanted to marry Betty. He said if I wouldn't want him to, then he wouldn't, but that he really wanted to. Once again, I couldn't voice what I really wanted to. I wanted to say, "*No,* don't marry her. I don't want you to do that." But I couldn't. I really didn't think he would really listen or hear me if I did speak my mind. He did what he wanted to. After all, he was an adult, and adults always do what they want. So I said that "It's all right with me. Go ahead and marry her." Dad seemed to be happy with her, and she was always nice to us kids. Betty told me that she *never* wanted to be one of those wicked stepmothers to us kids whom you always hear about. I was really glad to hear this. Now how weird is all of this? The kids whom I used to babysit with, and get paid to do it, are now part of my family. Sometime later, my dad adopted Betty's three kids, and now I instantly have two sisters and four brothers, whereas before I only had three brothers, and I had to babysit for free. Now how wrong is that? Now I was just a built-in babysitter without the pay. In the beginning of this combined family, everything seemed to be great. We all lived in Betty's house in a small town called Valley Center, Kansas, which is twelve miles north of Wichita, Kansas. I began my ninth-grade year of school there. The kids there seemed to be a little more accepting of me than in other schools. Some kids did stare at me and make fun of me, but mostly I was accepted.

The church that we attended was smaller than what I had been used to, but I liked it very well. The preacher of our church and his wife has three kids. The oldest, a son, is my age and very cute. I soon developed a crush on him. I was a fourteen-year-old teenager. Betty's oldest daughter, Kim, was only six years old. Betty was not used to dealing with a teenager on a daily basis. Here lies a major problem. My youngest brother, David, was three years old. He had been taken away from his mom. He was too young to understand what had happened to the family or where his mom was. David was a very needy child and acted out a lot. Who could blame him? I tried to help out with him as much as I could. We refer to Dad's wife as "Betty." That is her name and what we have called her since we have known her. One day, Melissa, Betty's youngest daughter, called her Betty, instead of Mom like she had heard us my brothers and I do. Betty became so furious that she insisted we all call her Mom from now on. The boys did, but I wouldn't. I have a mom, and she isn't her. I knew that, occasionally, I would slip and call her Mom and then hated myself when I did. We (my brothers and I) got to see our mom once in a while, but not often enough. Dad said it cost too much in gas to go to Fort Scott all the time, so the trips became few and far between. Mom came to see us some, but I didn't think Dad or Betty, especially Betty, liked or even wanted my mom at their house. Those visits eventually stopped. Mom would call us and send letters and cards, but those stopped also, and I didn't know why.

Time went by, and we were all in a routine. I shared a room with my sister Kim. It's not so bad, even though she was eight years younger than me. Betty had become very controlling now. Dad worked all the time. Betty worked for a while outside the home, then quit and opened up a state-licensed day care in the home. She had several kids that she babysat for during the day and then all of us at night. I thought all of this was wearing on her. She was no longer patient or understanding. She was frustrated and angry more and more. She went way overboard with discipline on the day care kids and on us. The day care lasted for about two years or so. She then got a job working at Beech Aircraft, where my dad worked. She was a secretary. Things really began to change at home then. David was in school then and quite a handful. Betty took David to a doctor, who said that he had allergies to just about every food that there was. She had a two-page list of and all foods he could no longer have. The list was so long that people wondered what foods he could have. David was also a bed-wetter. He got into trouble for it. If he wet the bed, then he didn't get any breakfast, because he had to get himself cleaned up (showered and dressed). Then he had to change all his bedding, by himself, and then make his bed. By the time he got everything done, it's time for school and no time for breakfast, and we were not allowed to help him. During lunchtime at school, he didn't get much to eat. Because of his so-called allergies, that I didn't believe he had, the school couldn't feed him much. He begged for food off other kids' trays because he was so hungry.

We all had to be home by a certain time right after school. Betty called at a certain time, and Kim was the only one allowed to answer the phone whenever Dad and Betty weren't home. If one of us was not there when Betty called, then that person was in big trouble. That person always seemed to be David. David was always being sent to bed without his dinner. If he brought home a bad report from the teacher, he got sent to bed with no dinner. If he forgot some of his homework, he got sent to bed with no dinner. If he was late getting home from school, he got sent to bed with no dinner. If he got into trouble in any way, he got sent to bed with no dinner. Some days, the only food and nourishment he got was lunch at school. He got no breakfast and no dinner. No wonder he was a problem child. He was starving not only for food but for love. You just don't punish a child by denying food and nutrition. It's just wrong. I snuck him some food when I could, but I was not always able to.

Betty had grown to hate David. I felt she hated his very existence. One night at dinner, when he actually got to have dinner, David got sick and threw up onto his plate. Betty got so angry at him that she told him that he had to eat the vomit off his plate. Dad actually stopped that and defended David. Dad told Betty to leave David alone, then took his plate to the sink emptied and cleaned it off, then fixed David a fresh plate of food to eat. Because Dad worked so much, he didn't know all the stuff that went on the house when he was gone. David got the blame for just about everything, even for things that he did not do. Betty whipped him a lot. I felt that she took her anger and frustration out on him. Whenever I tried to tell Dad some of what was going on at home, he said that I was just making things up because I didn't like Betty and that I was just trying to cause trouble for him and Betty. Well, the part about not liking Betty was true; I had grown not to like her. But what she was doing to David was true. Betty told us that our mom no longer loved us, or even cared about us. She said that if our mom did love us, she would call and or write to us, but she didn't. I guessed that Betty was right about that. Kim had become quite the tattletale in the house. She told her mom everything we said and or did; then all hell broke loose when Betty got home. It seemed to me that Betty's three kids could do no wrong and Dad's three kids could do no right. We attended church all the time and were involved in church activities. I was sure God did not approve of the way Betty treated us kids. In public, Betty acted like she cared about us, but behind closed doors, it's a very different story. I felt that we were simply tolerated and put up with because we are Dad's kids. I didn't believe that she wanted us in her life. Dad wanted us in his life, so Betty had to accept us for him. All she really wanted is my dad for herself and her kids; us kids just happened to come with him. Why didn't Dad see or listen to what was going on at home? I just didn't get it. What was going on inside of his head?

I really feared for David's health, and he developed asthma. Some of his spells were pretty bad. One spell was so bad that he asked me if I thought he was going to die. I promised him that he would not die, I would not allow it. He did survive that episode. He was so thin, his ribs were showing, and his eyes were sunken, and dark circles were underneath. He acted up more and more, which pushed Betty's buttons all the more. I had never one time ever seen Betty's three kids miss a single meal, not for any reason. But *we* sure had. For someone who never wanted to be a wicked stepmom, she sure became one. I was sixteen then and had taken driver's ed at school and got my driver's license. Dad took me car shopping. He bought for me a 1974 Oldsmobile Cutlass. He paid for it out of my settlement I received from my accident as a kid. My dad was the conservator of this account. When I started driving my car, I thought, at least I would have more freedom to get away from the house and Betty. Boy, was I ever wrong about that. Every time I wanted to go somewhere, I had to take one of the kids with me. Their choice was always Kim, the tattletale. I did take David once in a while and would buy him food sometimes when I had the money to do so. My car was used as leverage against me. Most kids my age could go and hang out with their friends, but not me. I had to always stay at home.

It's my junior year in high school, and time for our junior-senior prom. I was actually being allowed to go. I had a dress and everything. I didn't have a date, but that was all right. I was still going and very excited about it. I couldn't wait to get all dressed up and go. I had on a very ugly color of blue nail polish that I just had to remove. We were all out of nail polish remover, and Dad and Betty had gone out shopping, and I was home with all the kids. I ran right next door to the neighbor and asked to borrow some nail polish remover. I came right back home, sat down, and removed the ugly blue polish that I had on, then returned the remover right away, thanked the neighbor, and came back home right away. Later, when Dad and Betty returned home from shopping, Betty noticed that my blue polish had been removed and asked how I got it off. I told her that I borrowed some remover from the neighbor. She became so angry at me for having done that. She immediately grounded me from the prom and sent me to my room for the rest of the night, with no dinner, of course. My dad did nothing. While in my room, that

I shared with Kim, I was so angry and crying and talking to myself. Kim overheard me saying that her mom was a bitch. She then went and told Betty what I said. The next thing I knew was I was also grounded from my car for two weeks. I couldn't attend my prom over borrowed nail polish remover and was grounded from my car for two weeks for talking to myself about Betty that her Kim overheard and reported. My dad then said that I had to apologize to Betty for what I said. After I did, Betty refused to accept it, saying I didn't really mean it. She was right again; I didn't really mean it, especially since it was forced by my dad. I wanted to work part-time to earn extra money, but Dad said no. School was more important, so I was not allowed. I didn't do much babysitting outside of the house anymore. Most of the baby sitting was for my siblings. I never had any spending money of my own to do anything or go anywhere. Gas money was given to me strictly for school and running the kids somewhere. A time limit was put on every run made with my car, even to school and home. Summers were spent at the local swimming pool. The folks bought a family pool pass. I had to take the kids almost every day; it's part of my babysitting job, but I did enjoy it also, going to the pool that is. Summer was also corn-shucking time. Dad went to a farm and brought home a truckload of com. We spent all day shucking corn, while Betty was in the kitchen, cooking and blanching the com, then cutting it off the cob and bagging it up for the freezer. This was an entire weekend chore. We also went to Betty's parents' home. They lived on a farm down in southern Kansas. They were the most wonderful people in the world. I don't know how they have a daughter like her. Being around them made me really miss my own grandparents. I also really missed my aunt Betty and uncle Tom and spending time on their farm with my cousins. I didn't know if I would ever see any of them again in life. I guess that they are a part of my past now. Betty's parents were Grandma and Grandpa T. On their farm, they had lots of chickens used for slaughter. The little kids got to try and catch them and bring them to Dad. Dad then tied the chickens by one leg to a fence. After several were caught and tied up, he then went along and cut their heads off. After a while, the dead chickens were put into a huge pot of boiling water for only a few short minutes that Grandpa T had going. Then we older kids got to pluck off all the feathers from the chickens after they were pulled from the boiling water. After the feathers had been plucked, the chickens were taken into the house, where Betty and Grandma T gutted them and cleaned them and bagged them for the freezer. We took a lot of them home for our big family. I was a city kid, but I really didn't mind doing this. It was quite an experience, and I loved being on a farm. Another thing that we did as a family that I really loved to do and enjoy was camping. Dad bought a small camper. It's one of those that looked like a box. It all had to be opened up and could sleep maybe six, but we put nine in it.

My brother Robin was back here now and living with us. He sure had changed in looks, and his voice became much deeper then than it had been. He now said we couldn't call him Robin anymore. His name is just Rob. That took a while to get used to, because he had always been Robin to me. But I honored his wishes and called him just Rob. We didn't seem to fight as much as we used to. I guess because we were a little older and had been apart for two years. Anyway, the place that our family went camping at was called the "Hide Out." It's a very much hidden campground, hence the name Hide Out. There were a lot of activities to do there. This place was so cool. Dad did a lot of fishing and setting up trout lines. There were playgrounds and equipment for the younger kids. There were rope swings. One was for small kids, and one for big kids and adults. There were three-wheelers to rent and ride on. Rob and I rode on them around the course that was there for them. We had a blast on them. I really enjoyed this camping and roughing it stuff. One morning, when Dad had his trout lines out, he woke up Rob and told him to go and check the lines. A little while later, we heard Rob yelling and screaming for help. We all went to see what was wrong. We found Rob up on a big log that was sticking out of the water. He said that an alligator had chased him up onto the log. As it turned out, it was not an alligator; it was a fish call a gar, which also has large teeth. We cracked up laughing at Rob over that one; he was really scared.

Birthdays were really special in our house. The birthday person got to choose whatever they wanted for the meal. Whatever your favorite meal was got fixed for dinner. The younger kids always wanted hotdogs, or tacos, or pizza. My favorite meal was always Swiss steak. Betty was a wonderful cook. Everything she made was always homemade and from scratch. Her Swiss steak was to die for. When it came to cooking, there wasn't anything that she couldn't make. Her homemade noodles she made for pots of beef or chicken and noodles were the best. Then there was her baking. The woman could really bake. Again everything was from scratch. Her cakes and pies were wonderful. My favorites were her chocolate, banana cream, and coconut cream pies. The crusts were so flaky and tender; they just melted in your mouth. I did learn a lot about cooking from her; that was a good thing. Holiday baking was the best time. She made all kinds of cookies and sweetbreads and candies. We all helped in the shelling of the pecans. Sometimes, we ate more than what got put into the bowl. Holidays were my favorite time of the year, with all the food and music and decorations, not to mention all the baking. The house always smelled so good from all the cooking. My best friend, Lettie Smith, the one who went to the Osmond concert with me, had since moved away with her family to Louisiana. She wrote letters to me. I wrote her a letter once, telling her how bad things had gotten here with Betty and that I had considered ending my life but couldn't do it. I started cutting myself with a razor blade on my stomach. I put the letter in an envelope and sealed it. I asked Betty for a stamp to mail it. She told me that she would take care of it for me. She had met my friend Lettie and seemed to like her. A day or two later, Betty confronted me with my dad and asked to see the cuts that I had been making on myself. I denied knowing what they were talking about.

Then Betty told me that she had opened and read my letter to Lettie. That was how she knew I had been cutting myself. Nothing was sacred or personal in this house, not as long as she was around. I never wrote to anyone ever again, because she cannot be trusted. I had very few friends and couldn't go anywhere and could rarely have someone over. There was a girl at school who was really smart and good in school and was also an athlete and called me a friend. Her name was Patricia. She had offered to come to my house and help tutor me with my problem subjects from school. I asked Dad if it would be okay for her to come and help me, and he said *no* because she was a black person. He said that "If you let one come over, and then they all will want to come over." He said he was not prejudice, though. I couldn't tell Patricia the real reason she couldn't come over—just that I had to study harder on my own.

Dad said that I was too trusting and that it would get me into big trouble one day. He said that people like me with such disabilities are easy targets for people in the world to take advantage of. He said that I would be on my own someday and I would have to learn not to be so trusting of people. Yet it was he and my mom who taught us to trust adults and authority figures, the police, and our government and such. Now he said not to trust so much. So which is it? To trust or not to trust? That was a big question. Dad had sheltered and protected me so much from the world to a degree that I was almost scared at the thought of having to be on my own. I talked about wanting to get married someday. Dad said jokingly that on my wedding day when the minister asks, "If anyone objects to this union, speak now, or forever hold your peace," and if anyone speaks up, he would punch them in the mouth. He said that he was looking forward to my wedding day and walking me down the aisle, and our father-daughter dance at the reception.

Dad said that because I would be on my own one day that I would need to learn how to change a tire on my car. He said that I should not count on or trust someone to come along to help me should I have a flat tire. We went out to my car, and he worked with me until I can change the tire on my own. I did learn how to do it with one arm. I was truly proud of that accomplishment. I was able to get the lug nuts off using a four-way and able to get the tire out of the trunk and onto the car, and the lug nuts tightened back on. He also showed me how to change the oil and oil filter but didn't make me do that. Well, it was my senior year in high school. I was only in school for a half day. I was in a program at school that allowed us to attend school of a morning and work in the afternoon and still get credit for a whole school day. My job was at a clothing company called Henry's. I worked in the office in payroll. I did paperwork and learned payroll. That job lasted from September until just after

December, thru the holidays; then I got let go. In February, I got another job working at a laboratory. I worked in the office at the switchboard. I learned how to operate the PBX switchboard. There were so many buttons, but after a week or so, I had them all down. I also did filing of the medical reports that came in. I really enjoyed this job. I worked the second-shift hours, from 3:00 to 11:30 p.m. I still only went to school a half day even though I worked the night shift. At home, I was charged fifty dollars a month for rent and ten dollars a week for groceries. Dad and Betty said the rent I paid was to teach me that it had to be paid monthly should I have to move out on my own. They said that when I get ready to move out on my own, they would give me back what I paid them in rent. How cool was that. I was eighteen then. Dad came to me and said the money that I received from my accident as a child belonged to me. He then told me that he didn't think that I was mature enough to handle it or take care of it and said that I needed to go with him into court and ask the judge to extend the length of the conservatorship to my age of twenty-one. Because I believed that my dad did what was in my best interest, I agreed to do so. Dad and Betty came to me yet again to talk about my mom. Once again, Betty said that if my mom truly loved and cared about me, she would contact me in some form, through letters or phone calls or visits, but nothing, and my dad agreed. Then Betty continued to say how much she loved me and that she had always been there for me. Then she said that she would like to adopt me. They said since I was eighteen, I could sign for myself and didn't need my mom's permission to do so. She and Dad talked me into this idea of theirs. We got into court, and I signed the papers in front of a judge, stating that I wished for Betty to adopt me and become my legal mother. After we got home, Betty suggested and insisted that I call my mom and tell her the news, that she was no longer my mother. Betty insisted that I tell my mom that she (Betty) was my new mom. I didn't really want to do that, but once again, Betty pushed me to do so. Since I didn't know how to get a hold of my mom, Dad said to call my grandma and find out. When I called my grandma, I was excited to talk to her. I really missed my grandma. Grandma said that Mom was in the hospital and gave me the number and room. Grandma said Mom would be glad to hear from me. I thought, *No, she won't because of what I have to tell her.* I hung up the phone and told Dad and Betty that Mom was in the hospital and that I couldn't call her at this time and give her this news. Betty said, "Sure you can. There is no better place for her to be when she hears the news." Betty said that if my mom collapsed, then she would be where she could get help. I thought, *How coldhearted can this woman be? What have I done? I am so gullible and easily manipulated. I just can't seem to stand up for myself or speak up for myself, and Betty definitely takes advantage of that too. My mom may not care about me, but I don't want to hurt her.* Betty made me call my mom anyway and tell her the news. Mom started crying and dropped the phone, and then Betty told me to hang up the phone, and I did. I couldn't believe that I just did that. I was becoming just as mean as Betty, and as hateful too. I didn't like myself very much then. I didn't want to be this way.

Well, time passed, and it was my graduation day, May of 1976. I wished my mom could be there to watch me graduate, but that was not to be. There were all kinds of graduation parties being held by some of my classmates that night. I was not allowed to attend any of them per Dad and Betty's orders. They had a small celebration at home for me, and I got a set of luggage as a gift. They said that I must move out that summer. Well, I was currently looking for an apartment. Betty came home one afternoon from work and said she found an apartment for me in Wichita that she said I could afford. It's a one-bedroom basement apartment with its own side entrance and was partially furnished with a bed and dresser, stove and refrigerator, couch and chair with a coffee table and end tables, and even pictures on the walls. All I needed were dishes, cookware, bedding, and a TV. I spoke to the landlord, and the apartment was mine. However, it was being redone, and I couldn't move in for about six weeks. A month had gone by, and there were about two weeks before the big move. One Friday night, after I got off work, I decided to stop at our local "eighteen" bar called Preston's, that was a few blocks from home in Valley Center, Kansas. They were open until 1:00 a.m. I got off work at 11:30 p.m. and drove the thirty miles back home to Valley Center. I arrived at the bar at about midnight. I was not a drinker but wanted to visit with some of my friends. I was sitting there, drinking a Coke and chatting with my friends when, all of a sudden, my dad and Betty came walking in. They hauled me out of there, telling me that I had disgraced and shamed the family for being in a bar. I tried to explain to them that I had not been drinking anything but a cola. I told them to smell my breath to see that I was telling the truth. I just wanted to unwind and visit with my friends. I wasn't doing anything wrong. They just wouldn't listen. Then Betty informed me that I had to be out of the house the very next day. I told her that I could not move in for another two weeks. She said that she didn't care, that I had better call the landlady and tell her that I couldn't wait the two weeks. That next morning (Saturday), I called the landlady and explained that I could not wait the last two weeks, and the landlady okayed me to move into the apartment that day. Dad and Betty didn't speak to me the whole day as I loaded up my car with my things. Dad put the rest of my things in the back of his truck, and off to the apartment we went. Betty had said that Dad was not going to help me move, but he did anyway. I knew that that probably pissed her off, but I didn't care. Dad and I got my things all moved into my apartment, and then he left. There I was, all alone, in my first very own place, scared and excited all at the same time. I decided that since I was nineteen and living on my own, and no one could tell me what to do, I would go out tonight. After all, it was a Saturday night. I was going to go back to Valley Center to Preston's, the eighteen bar, and visit with my friends, and told myself I would to stay there until the bar closed at 1:00 a.m. This time, no one could haul me out of there. I got some of my things put away and then took a shower and was getting all dressed up to go out when, all of a sudden, Dad and Betty and all my brothers and sisters showed up. With them, they brought groceries, cookware, and other things. They said that they were going to spend the first evening with me in my new apartment. I just couldn't believe this. I thought, *This has got to be a set up. I am living on my own in my very own apartment. Betty doesn't even like me. She couldn't wait to get me out of the house, and now she wants to spend the evening with me? What is even worse is she acts like the last twenty-four hours never happened.* However, once again, I hadn't the guts to say anything. We had a somewhat enjoyable evening, and they left around 10:00 p.m. I waited for about thirty minutes after they had gone before I left to go to the bar. I feared that they were parked somewhere watching me. I left anyway and went to the bar. This time, no one could haul me out of the bar. I decided to stay until 1:00 a.m. and have fun. My only worry was David. I thought, *Who will look after him? Who will protect him from Betty? Who will sneak food to him? I cannot worry about that right now. It feels so good not to have a curfew or anyone telling me what I can and cannot do. I might even stay out all night long.*

Eventually, I got settled into my place and a routine. I go to work and come home. Sometimes, I go out after work. I still drove back to Valley Center every Sunday for church. I was afraid that if I was not in church on Sunday, my dad would show up at my place and give me what for. I frequently went to the bar on Saturday night but was at church on Sunday morning. I still feared my dad's wrath, but I was on my own, so what's with that? I continued the churchgoing for about three months until I got the nerve to stop going to see if my dad showed up at my apartment. You know what? He did not show up. How cool was that. So I quit going from then on. I thought I could truly live my life on my own terms. While working at the lab, I met a girl who would turn out to be my lifelong best friend. Her name is Debbie. We seemed to hit it off instantly. We started hanging out together. We went places together and just had fun. Debbie and I started going to an all-night diner called Kings X after work to get a bite to eat and relax. The diner was only a couple of blocks from my house. There I met a man who would become my first boyfriend. His name is Rod. He really liked me. We always met up at the diner after work. He also worked second shift but at another company. He was so wonderful and really cute. He never tried anything with me, sexually that is. I really liked that about him because I was not ready for that yet. I did tell him that I was a virgin, and he thought that that was all right and said he wouldn't pressure me into anything, and he didn't. We spent every waking minute together. He came to my apartment a couple of hours before we both had to go to work so we could spend time together; then we got together after work and went bowling or down to the river just to watch the sun come up. Sunrises had never been as beautiful as they were with him. We really just enjoyed each other's company. We sometimes just sat together for hours and said nothing at all. I had never felt this way before. Could it be love? I thought so. I thought I was falling in love with him. I just knew that I wanted to spend forever with him. Then he told me that he loved me. Oh my goodness, he loved me, and I told him that I loved him also. Life just couldn't get any better than this. He even told me that one day he would like to marry me. Well, one night after work we were with some other people, and one of the girls he worked with pulled me off to the side and told me that she knew that Rod and I were getting serious and just wanted me to know that he was a married man. I was in total shock, and I didn't believe her. I told her it's not true, that she was just lying because she was jealous of what Rod and I had. She said to ask him. So I did, and he admitted to me that it was true and that he also had three children. He said that he hadn't been happy in his marriage for a long time. He said that he loved me and wanted to be with me. I just couldn't believe this. I had to get away from him. I couldn't be with him. He belonged to someone else. He said that he wouldn't let me go. I told him that he had to. He called and came by my place for weeks afterward, but eventually the calls and everything stopped. How do I get past this hurt? I loved him so much I just wanted to die. I called Debbie and started hanging with her again. We spent time at her place and mine. I even took her out to the house to meet Dad and Betty and the kids. I was not so sure that they liked Debbie. Debbie is five years older than me and was very outspoken and always spoke her mind regardless. I didn't think Betty liked that, and I really didn't care. I myself was reserved and quiet, and didn't speak up; Debbie just said it like it was. I wished that I could be more like her. I thought that was what Dad and Betty were afraid of.

Debbie was also an Elvis Presley fan, and we found out that Elvis was coming to town to give a concert. Well, we decided that we were both going to go to this concert for sure. The day finally came for the concert, and we were really excited and couldn't wait to see him. Our seats happened to be up in what we called the nosebleed section. Debbie had a pair of high-powered binoculars that we watched him through. Oh my God, he put on a fantastic concert. He (Elvis) had put on a lot of weight, but he still looked great and could still shake it like he always did. What a fabulous concert. I couldn't wait to see him again one day. Fat or not, he still had it.

One day, out of the blue, I got a phone call from a lady friend of the family. Her name was Marty. Betty used to babysit her son Glen—in the day care she had years earlier. Marty's husband, Gary, had died, and she said that she was tired of mourning the loss and wanted to go out and asked me to go with her. I said sure, and we went to a restaurant/bar called Scotch & Sirloin. She ordered a drink, and I had a cola. We were just sitting there talking when this man and a group of people with him came walking in. Marty saw this man and said, "Oh my God."

She said to me, "Do you know who that man is?" I looked at him and didn't know him or any of the other people with him. So I asked who he was, and she said he was the "only the man that her brothers (all in law enforcement) had been trying to arrest for years." She said that the law couldn't get enough evidence to ever arrest him. So I asked her about him, "Who is he, and what does the law think he has done?" She said his name is George and that he was in the Mafia and had done all kinds of illegal things, but nothing could be pinned in him. The only thing that I knew about the Mafia was what I had seen in the movie *The Godfather*. The Mafia, from what I know, is not a people you want to mess with. I wasn't even sure that they existed in real life. Marty said, "Yes, they are very real people." The next thing she said was that she was going to buy that man a drink. She then motioned for the waitress. The waitress came over, and Marty told her that she wanted to order that man—and she pointed him out—a drink. A few minutes later, the waitress came back and said that George would only accept the drink if he could come sit with us and drink it. I quickly said *no*, but Marty, of course, said, yes, he could. I protested once more to Marty, but she wouldn't listen. "Here he comes," Marty told me not to mention to him what I knew about him. "Don't worry," I said. I didn't want him to know that I knew he probably killed people for a living. I was really scared then. I was afraid that if I looked at him wrong or said the wrong thing that he might decide to have me killed or a contract put on me.

Marty had completely lost her mind, and she was going to take mine with her. I decided to just sit there, quiet as a mouse while they talked. Eventually, he asked me what I did for a living. I told him that I worked at Beech Aircraft. By this time, I had switched jobs from the lab to Beech Aircraft. So stupid me, I asked him what he did for a living. I wanted to grab those words right out of the air as soon as they left my mouth, but it was too late. He replied, "I do a little of this and a little of that." I knew exactly what he meant. He also said that he travelled back and forth from Las Vegas all the time. In my mind, the trips to and from Las Vegas were for covering up the money he got paid to do his illegal jobs. I didn't like this man, and I didn't want to be around him, but I rode with Marty and had no way to leave. I was pretty sure that Marty wouldn't let anything happen to me, but I was scared just the same. After a while, he (George) said that the party would continue at his apartment. He asked if we would like to come. I said, "No, thank you," but Marty said, yes, we would come. After we got to the car, I told Marty that I did not wish to go and for her to take me home. She said no, that she was really turned on by him and wanted to go to his place but wouldn't go alone and that I was going with her. I argued, but it did no good. A little while later, we arrived at his place. It's a very fancy and large apartment. Once inside the door, the dining room and kitchen were to the left; to the right was the living room. I felt somewhat safer because a lot of other people were there. All I wanted to do was go home. I didn't have any money for a cab, and Marty insisted that I stay with her. This man was old enough to be my father; he was divorced and had a daughter. He tried to talk to me, and I spoke only to answer him. A while later, Marty started making out with him, and eventually they went to the bedroom.

After a while, everyone else left, and I was all alone in the living room. After a while, I finally dozed off in the big square chair that I was sitting in. A few hours later, I got awakened by Marty. She said it's time to leave, and so we left. I told her that I could not believe what she got us into. She said that she was even more turned on than before. She said that her brothers would just die if they knew whom she had been with and that they could never find out. She intended on seeing him again. I, on the other hand, didn't ever intend on seeing him again, with or without her. Later, I told Debbie what happened. Debbie knew who George was and told me to stay as far away as I could get from him. Debbie said that he could be a very dangerous man. I told her that staying away from him was definitely my intention.

After a year in my first apartment, I decided to move because I discovered that my landlady's daughter had been letting herself into my place with her mom's master key when I was gone and taking some of my things. I found a small one-bedroom rental house across town from where I was. I rented it and got moved in and settled. It's a real nice place, and it's a house, not an apartment, a major plus. I really liked it. Debbie and I continued to hang out and have fun. We found a country western bar that we really enjoyed going to. The place was called the Wagon Wheel. We went there every weekend to dance. We both loved to dance. We danced by ourselves, we danced together, and we danced with almost everyone else there. We were always together. People referred to us as each other's sidekick. The bartender there and I were seeing each other. After a while, I find out that he was married. His wife suspected that he was seeing someone and confronted Debbie outside the bar one weekend with a .44 handgun, thinking that she was the one sleeping with her husband. Debbie said that she didn't know what she was talking about, and if her husband was being unfaithful, he was not doing it with her but she would keep her eyes open for her. The wife didn't suspect me and didn't bother Debbie anymore either. Not long after that, I quit seeing him, because I did not want to end up dead should she find out about me, and it's wrong anyway. Deb and I decided that going to the clubs every weekend was getting a little expensive, so we discovered that we both like camping. We put together some equipment and started spending weekends camping out at Lake Afton outside of town. We had a blast camping. We met some real cool people out there. Every weekend, there were the regulars who came out. We all hung out together. That was where I met the next man in my life, Jim.

Jim was an older man; he worked at Boeing Aircraft and was divorced, with one son. Jim and I started dating. I introduced him to Dad and Betty. They liked him quite well. We dated for about a year and then broke up.

One day, I was out at Dad and Betty's house, visiting. Dad wasn't there this particular time. I witnessed Betty's son Steven did something that he shouldn't have. When Betty found out and asked who did it, Steven immediately spoke up and said that David did it. I then spoke up and said, no, David didn't do it, that Steven had done it. Steven started crying and saying that he did not do it, and he even promised that he did not do it, and Betty believed him, naturally because he was her son. She got really angry and grabbed a belt and swung it buckle end out at David and hit him with the buckle. I screamed at her and told her that David didn't do it. Steven was crying and saying that David did do it. Betty said that her children didn't lie and that I was just trying to protect my brother from being punished. I told her that that was true; I was trying to protect my brother, but he did not do it, that her own son did it and that I saw it myself. She swung the belt a second time with the buckle end out, and I stood up and caught the belt in midair and grabbed it from her and shoved her backward onto the couch. She started yelling at me, telling me that she was going to tell my dad that I put my hand on his wife and, when he found out, there would be hell to pay; and I knew that that was true, but I had to protect my brother. In my anger, I told her to go ahead and tell my dad, because I had a few things to tell him myself about what went on there. So we waited for Dad to come home. We waited and waited and waited. It got late, and I had to leave and go home. I got David all tucked into bed, and then I left. I went home and waited some more for Dad. He never showed up, probably because it was so late. The very next day after work, I went straight home to wait for Dad, because I know he had heard the story by now and would confront me for sure today. I waited and waited some more. Dad never showed up. I was really puzzled by this. The next day was the same, no Dad. The only thing that I could figure was that Betty didn't tell Dad about the fight she and I had. She didn't tell him that I shoved her onto the couch. I knew for a fact that if she had told him, he would have confronted me and since I hadn't seen hide nor hair of him, she never said a word. She was afraid of me and what I would tell him. I didn't know if he would even believe me. I had tried to tell him things in the past, and he either didn't believe me or just turned a blind eye to it; I just don't know which. Not long after that episode, I once again was out at the house visiting, really just checking on David, when, all of a sudden, "my" mother showed up. I was totally stunned. I couldn't believe she was here. *Why is she here?* I wondered. Betty said that Mother was here to pick up David and take him to live with her. David instantly recognized our mother and ran up to her and grabbed her and hugged her and then heard her say, "Hi, little boy, what is your name?" I saw the look on David's face; he was crushed. Our own mom didn't recognize her own son. He was so thin and pale and had dark circles under his eyes; you could even see his ribs because he was so malnourished. I wanted so badly to go to my mom, but I couldn't. I was afraid to because of what Dad and Betty made me say to her years earlier. I didn't know if she hated me or not; I would hate me if I was her, but I was too scared to find out. I was so happy for David, though. No, that was not true; I was thrilled and overjoyed for him. I knew now that he would live and be loved and *fed*, and he would thrive. Thank you, God, for this. I couldn't help but wonder what brought this all about, though. Betty must have decided to let David go before things went too far. Didn't matter anymore then. David would be safe and happy. Life started becoming great; I had no more worries about David. Some time went by, and I got a phone call from Dad. He said that he wanted to talk to me about my settlement money—the money he took care for me until I was twenty-one. I went out to the house, and Dad sat me down and said that he would like to borrow the money from me. I asked him how that could happen since I didn't have it to begin with. Dad said that we have to go back into court and tell the judge that I want my money and that I didn't want to wait until I was twenty-one. Dad said not to mention to the judge that he intended to borrow the money from me. He said that that was to be between him and me and that the judge didn't need to know about it. I told Dad that it was okay, I would loan him the money. So to court we went. When the judge handed me the check for some $29,000, the last thing he said to me was, "Do not to spend it all in one place." I said I wouldn't and thanked him, and then Dad and I left. Once outside, I handed the check over to Dad. Dad said that he would begin to repay the money back in six months with $100 savings bonds until it was paid back in full. I said okay and that I trust him and believe him. Anyway, life went on, and Dad and Betty bought a new house a couple of blocks away from the old house that we all lived in once. They also bought a new truck and furnished the new house with new things, and even put a pool table in the newly finished basement. It really was a nice place they had there. My friend Debbie and I went out and visited from time to time, and Debbie even played a few games of pool with my dad.

A few months went by, and out of the blue, I ran into that George guy. I was polite but went on my way. A few weeks later, he showed up at my house. I asked him how he knew where I lived; he said he got my address thru my license plate number at the DMV. He told me that he knew I had had some difficulties in my life. He said that he was aware of a certain financial problems that I was having. He then handed me an envelope with $5,000 cash inside. I asked what it's for. He said it was to pay off all of the bills that he knew I had and get myself out of debt. He said that he had me checked out so he knew I could use the money. I proceeded to tell him that I couldn't accept the money. He said, "Sure you can." I said, no, I couldn't. He then asked why not. I answered because I could never repay that amount of money. He then said I would not have to repay it. I said, yes, I would but couldn't. He said, no, I would not. All I would have to do for him would be to pick up and deliver a few packages every now and then without asking any questions. I didn't know how or why, but I just knew that I did not want to be tied to this man in any way for any reason, and I did not want to be a part of that group of people. So I very politely refused the money so as not to make him angry at me. The next thing he said to me shocked more than I could ever have imagined. I didn't know how he got his information, but he somehow knew about the problems that I had been having with Betty. He said to me that he could and would have that particular problem permanently eliminated from my life. I hate to admit that I really had to think about that one. I knew exactly what he meant by the word *eliminate*. I hate to admit it, but a part of me really wanted to say yes, but I just couldn't. I didn't know it then, but my belief in God and the Bible just would *not* let me say yes to him. Because I have a conscience, Betty is alive today. Because I have a conscience, Betty's children have their mother. Because I have a conscience, my dad still has his wife. I knew that George wanted to use me in his dealings because no one would ever suspect a handicapped person like me being a runner for him and his kind. Betty had no idea how close she came to not being here anymore, but she is still here because I had a conscience. Then George left my house, and I never saw or heard from him again. When I told my friend Debbie all that happened with George, she said that refusing that money was one of the best decisions I ever made, and didn't I know it. After a few months, one of my bosses at work (and I had two of them) told me that I had been given my two weeks' notice, that I had been fired. I was in total shock. I couldn't believe this was happening to me. The boss that I liked and respected gave me this news. His name was Gene. He later called into his office and told me to fight this termination. I told him that I didn't know how. He suggested that I go and speak with the vice president of our department and tell him everything I knew about what was going on. The "everything" was that I found out that Betty and my other boss who didn't like me worked together to get me fired, and they succeeded in doing so.

So I took Gene's advice and made an appointment with the VP Mr. Harold D. I told him everything including what I had been told about Betty and my other boss Tom F and how they had conspired to get me fired. He told me to give him a few days to investigate things and that he would get back to me. A few days later, Mr. Harold D informed me that my termination had been cancelled and that I would be working directly for him doing special projects. Wow, how cool was that. Now that I had saved my job, I gave Betty a call at her office and told her to meet me at my apartment right after work. By God, she really showed up. I told her that I knew about her and my boss Tom F's scheme to get me fired. I also informed her that it did no good, that I still had my job and got promoted also. I also told her that I knew she was behind my dad wanting to borrow my settlement money. She then told me that the money wasn't borrowed and that I would never see any of that money ever again. She said that I couldn't prove that I didn't spend it all myself.

Well, she was right about one thing. I didn't have any proof that I loaned the money to my dad. I did, however, tell her that my lawyer said we could prove that all the new things they bought—such as the new house, new truck, new furnishings, pool table, etc.—came real close to the amount of money that I had than what they could afford on their own with their income. Besides, if I had spent the money myself, I would have something to show for the money, such as a new car, a new house, a new wardrobe to die for; I would definitely have something to show for $29,000. I didn't but they do. She then asked me for the name of my lawyer, but I told her that was none of her business. She then asked what I planned on doing. I told her that my lawyer and I planned on taking her and my dad to court to get my money back. Betty then told me that I cannot prove anything, and that it was her word against mine, and that she would deny this entire conversation. At that moment, I walked over to a drawer that was slightly ajar, reached into it, and pushed the stop button on the recorder that had been on since she arrived. I also hit the eject button and pulled out the cassette that was inside of the machine and told her that I had all the proof I needed right there on this tape and in her own words. She tried to grab the tape, but she didn't get it from me. I was hanging on to this. Betty then left my apartment but not before I told her that I would get my money back and that I want her to stay completely out of my life. I could only imagine what lies she would tell my dad. I thought *I would just have to wait and see what happens.* A couple hours or so later, I got a phone call from Ruth, my sister-in-law, wanting to know what I had said to Betty that had her so upset. I asked her what she meant, and she told me that Betty had just left their place in tears saying something about me taking her to court. I told her everything that had happened. A few weeks later, my dad called me and told me to meet him at the courthouse. He was returning all of my money but had another conservatorship set up with a bank as the conservator, and I agreed and signed the papers just to get my money back. After a while, I decided to spend some of the money. I gathered up all my bills and took them to that bank and informed them that I wanted to have the bills paid off out of my money, and the bank did so.

I had begun to notice something about my body. Something was just not right. I noticed that my right breast was much larger, noticeably larger than my left one. I went to a doctor, and he said that I definitely had a lump in there and wanted to do surgery right away. He scheduled the surgery for the next day. He called it a biopsy. I got checked into to the hospital a few hours later. Debbie was with me and kept telling me that everything would be all right. I wanted to believe her, but with everything else that I had gone through in my life, I was just not so sure. Surgery was set for first thing in the morning. Debbie said she would be back in the morning to be with me and to try to relax. Yeah right. Well, the next morning came, and I was getting prepped for surgery. The nurses did an EKG on me, and when I asked what it's for, they told me that the doctor ordered it but that sometimes they didn't think he (the doctor) stopped to realize the age of his patients. My EKG was normal. Then they brought in some forms for me to sign. One of the forms said that I gave my permission to remove my breast if it turns out to be cancerous. Oh my God!

Do they think it is cancer? They said that while I was still out on the OR table, a biopsy of the lump would be tested, and if the test came back positive, then they would remove the breast at that time. I told them that I prefer to be awakened so that I could process the bad news if there was any before I have my breast removed. They told me that it didn't work that way—that there isn't any point to being opened up twice and operated on. If the news is bad, then one surgery would be enough because they would already be in there. I guess I understood their reasoning, so I agreed and signed the papers. This was the first time ever in my life that I was going into surgery, and my dad was not there with me. Debbie was there, but it's just not the same without my dad. He had always been with me whenever I was in the hospital. I was really scared then. I was all alone. I was going into surgery with two breasts, but I didn't know if I would have two when I wake up after. I woke up later in the recovery room very groggy. I, then, was transferred back to my room. Debbie was there waiting for me and began to talk to me. I started to cry and just assumed that they took my breast off.

Debbie reassured me that I still have both of my breasts. She said that the test showed the lump was benign, not cancerous. I really began to cry then because it was such a relief. I was in so much pain. Every fiber of my body hurt. From my neck down, I couldn't even raise my head up off the pillow. The doctor came in and said that I must have been so tense (*You think?*) when I went into surgery and was put out that it affected all my muscles, and that's why I was so stiff and sore. The doctor ordered not only pain relievers but also muscle relaxers. After two or three days, I got released from the hospital, and Debbie took me home. After a few weeks, I was healing nicely but had this scoop in my breast and a large scar where the doctor said would be a pencil line scar. More scars, that's just all I needed, as if I didn't have enough of them already. The doctor asked me if I have any family history of fibroids, because that was what I had, and I told him not that I know of. I didn't recall hearing anyone talking about them. I would sometime later find out that my grandma (Mom's mom) had them and had several of them removed; all were benign. A few months later, Debbie met a wonderful man named Lynn. They fell in love, got married, and moved away.

Well, I ended up moving again, too, to yet another place. This time, I was living in a mobile home in a mobile home park. I took a fall at work and was unable to work for a while. I ended up living on some of that settlement money because I had quit my job at Beech. I had been thinking a lot about my mom and really missing her. I didn't know if she would ever speak to me after what I did, but I just had to find out. One day, I finally got up enough nerve and called her mom, my grandma.

Grandma was thrilled to hear from me, and I was a little shocked but glad. I told her how very sorry I was for what I did to my mom years earlier or rather what I was forced to do. Grandma told me that Mom never held anything against me and that she still loved me and would very much like a relationship with me. I told my grandma that I was coming to visit the very next weekend. She said they would all plan for it. I didn't think that next weekend would ever get here. It did come, and I made the trip from Wichita to Fort Scott to see my grandparents and my mom and other relatives whom I hadn't seen in years. I had missed them more than words could say. Tears, a lot of tears, really flowed that weekend by everyone. A lot of information really came out also from both sides, theirs and mine. The real burning question I asked was why mom didn't contact us all those years ago. Why didn't she call, write, or come and visit? I was stunned by the answer. She did try to call and was told that we could not talk, we were grounded from the phone, or we simply were not there. Letters were sent by her and Grandma. They both sent birthday cards and Christmas cards with money inside. They assumed we had gotten them, but we never did. They even sent us Christmas presents that were returned to them unopened. They were also told by Betty not to come and visit because she would have them arrested for trespassing. We kids didn't know any of these. Betty simply refused us any contact with our mother, then told us that our mom did not love us. Betty had been lying to us for years, and we never even knew it. Since we kids were never allowed to answer the phone or get the mail, we never knew about the letters and cards and phone calls. Mom and Grandma said after a while they gave up trying and figured that they would just have to wait until we were grown and contacted them on our own. Mom told me that the day I called her and told her of my adoption by Betty that it was really Betty speaking thru me. Mom said that no piece of paper would ever change the fact that she was my mom and always would be.

That weekend was certainly an eye-opener for all of us, but mostly me. Everything made sense to me now. Betty never wanted any of us to know that our mom *did* try to contact her children. I hated Betty so much for what she had done to our family, and us kids. She was such a liar. I did have to say, though, that David looked wonderful. He had put weight on, and the dark circles were gone, and he was glowing from happiness and love from being with his mom. All the foods that Betty said David was allergic to was not

45

true. Mom said that she slowly introduced all of the foods to him, everything that was on the list of allergy foods, and he had absolutely no reaction to any of them. She also took him to a doctor, and he was given a clean bill of health, with no allergies to anything. David was thriving, and I could not be happier. All the information that I got that weekend made me almost wish that I had taken George up on his offer to eliminate that problem from "all" of our lives. I was so glad about the reconnection with my mom and grandparents and Aunt Betty and Uncle Tom. I love them all and have missed them so very much. We would never be separated again except in death.

After returning to Wichita, I kept thinking about all I learned and decided that I want Betty out of my life. I went and talked to an attorney about getting myself "unadopted." I explained to him how it all happened and told him that I wished to sign whatever papers necessary to become unadopted from this horrible person. The attorney informed me that it couldn't be done and that it was just unheard of and I would just have to live with it. Well, that just stinks, and once again, Betty won. Well, life went on, and I kept in touch with my mom and went to visit when I could. I was now very much separated from my dad. We didn't see or speak to each other. The last time I called out to the house to talk to him, Betty answered the phone and told me that Dad didn't want to talk to me. She told me that I was not welcome there anymore, and if I had to show up, she would have me arrested for trespassing. I tried to call many times over the next months and year or two. Betty always answered the phone. She said that Dad wasn't there, or he was sleeping or that he just didn't want to talk to me. I bet he didn't even know that I had been calling. I wondered what lies she had told him about me. Why didn't he try to reach out to me? Why didn't Dad just tell me himself that he didn't want anything to do with me? I wondered if she was pulling the same thing on Dad that she pulled on us kids. She was probably telling him that I didn't want anything to do with him or telling him that if I cared, I would call or come see him, but what he didn't know was that I had tried. I'd just stayed away, thinking maybe one day things would change. Dad could find me if he truly wanted to. He obviously didn't want to, because there was no contact from him. I just didn't understand what kind of man who used to be a good and loving father turns his back on his children all because of a woman. Betty had now what she obviously always wanted. She had my dad for herself and her children. Rob had gotten married and moved out, David was living with Mom, and I was out. Joe was the only one left there of Dad's kids. I wondered how he was being treated by Betty. Was he being deprived of food and or being beaten? I had no way of finding out either. I just had to trust that all was well and hope that he survived. I later found out that they moved again. They moved about an hour East of Wichita to live in the country by a river. I'd never been there and not allowed to come either, per Betty's orders. Well, time passed, and I discovered a new club to go to called the Brookside. It's a real nice and upscale place. I really enjoyed this place. They had a live band that played every weekend. Occasionally, they had different talents come in. One particular Saturday night, they had a woman psychic come in and give readings to people. I never believed in those kinds of people but told my friend that I was curious and paid the twenty dollars to have a private reading. I took nothing in with me and decided I would say nothing so I wouldn't give her any hints as to what to say to me. She started off by taking my hand. A minute or so later, she told me that I would be buying a car in the near future. I knew right away that that was a lie, because I had a perfectly good car and was not going to buy another one; however, I said nothing. Then she said that she saw me traveling west. I spoke up then and asked her what she meant by west. Did she mean west Wichita, west Kansas, or West Coast? She just said west was all she saw. *Okay, whatever*, I thought. Then she asked me if the name Charlie meant anything to me. I thought about it and answered no. The only Charlie I knew was an uncle. Then she said that she saw a man in my life with the name of Charlie or possibly Chuck or Charles. Then she said that she saw me raising a little girl by myself. Still I said nothing. A few minutes later, the session ended, and she wished me well, and I returned to my friend. I told my friend everything the woman said. We joked about it and went on with our evening. Sometime later, some friends of mine (a young couple with four kids) were separating, and she (Connie) asked me if her husband (Jack) could rent the spare bedroom I had in my trailer home. I said sure, and he moved in shortly thereafter. They only had one car and he let her keep it to take the kids back a forth to school. I started taking him to work and picking him up. His kids came over on the weekends and stayed with him. Then the next thing I knew was that one by one, the kids started moving in with him in my home. They didn't want to live with her anymore. In a matter of a few months, he and all four kids were living in my house. Now I was taking Jack to work and the two older kids to school and babysitting the two younger ones (not school-age yet). I got tired of taking Jack to and from work, so he asked me if I could help him buy a cheap car and that he would pay me back as soon as he can. So I did buy him a $900 car. Several months went by, and Jack and Connie had been trying to work things out between them. One day, they came to me and told me that they had job opportunities out in Denver, Colorado. I said that's great. Then they asked me if I could keep their kids until they get settled there. I didn't know why, but I said yes. The four kids were three boys and one girl. The girl was the number 2 child and was six years old. One day, a few weeks later, she got real sick, so sick that I had to take her to the hospital. She was admitted because she was very dehydrated and vomiting and also had diarrhea. She was one very sick little girl. I found out that Connie had a sister in town whom I took the boys to so that I could stay with the girl at the hospital. However, I wondered why the sister didn't agree to keep the kids. I couldn't worry about that then. I tried to get a hold of Jack and Connie but was not able to. A few days later, they called the hospital and talked to me there. I guessed the sister got a hold of them. Anyway, they came back and took the kids with them back to Colorado. They gave me their address and phone number. They lived in and managed a hotel there. They said they would send me money as soon as they could for the car I bought and others things I bought as well. I want to believe them, but I didn't. In August 1980, I decided take a trip to Denver, Colorado, to either collect the car or the money these people owed me. Upon arrival at the airport, I called the number they gave me, and Jack answered the phone. I told him I was at the airport in Denver and to please come and get me. He did so and took me back to the hotel where they lived and also managed. It's a fairly decent place. They got me set up into one of the rooms. At first, I told them that I was just there for a visit. While in Denver, I met a man named Rick Taylor. We had an instant attraction to each other. We spent the next three days together. He was so different from anyone I'd ever met.

On the third day, he told me that he loved me and asked me to marry him. I couldn't believe he was asking me that question. I always dreamed of hearing that question but wondered if I really ever would. Wow, I told him that I loved him, too, and, yes, I would marry him. He said he wanted to get married as soon as we could. We set the date for November 8. Not much time to plan a wedding, just a little over two months, but I knew I could do it. I called my mom to told her the news, and she was surprised but very happy for me. She said she would help in any way she could. I just knew then that I was getting married and my dad would be back in my life. After all, he had to walk me down the aisle like he said he would. I just knew that my wedding would bring us back together. A couple more days later, I returned to Wichita, only to find out that my place had been broken into and robbed. This was just great; I lost my TV and my stereo. There wasn't much else to take. Well, I couldn't think about that then. I had a wedding to plan. I ordered and put a rush on the invitations and went and bought my wedding dress. I asked Rick about his family, his mom and dad. He said that they weren't on speaking terms, and he wouldn't invite them to the wedding. He wouldn't even tell me their names so that I could invite them. He also had a sister, but I didn't know who she was either. For whatever reason, he just wouldn't talk about his family. I was so excited to tell my dad the news, and I kept trying to call him, but Betty always answered and said that he couldn't come to the phone or he wasn't there. She always had a reason I couldn't talk to him. I wanted to tell him my news. I finally told Betty my news so that she could tell my dad. She told me that my dad would not be attending my wedding. I thought, *How could she say that? How could she speak for him?* I just knew that she wouldn't even tell him that I had been calling, much less tell him that I was getting married and need him to walk me down the aisle on my wedding day. I asked myself how I was going to get a hold of my dad. I couldn't go to the house, and I couldn't get a hold of him on the phone. So I just planned to send him an invitation with a note in it to his work.

Meanwhile, Rick and I travelled to Fort Scott to talk to my mom and grandma about wedding plans. Grandma got someone she knew to make the cake. Granddad and Grandma offered their place for the wedding reception. The wedding itself would take place in a small country church in Richards, Missouri. Rick and I went to Nevada, Missouri, and got our license. I chose Missouri because getting married didn't require a blood test. I really didn't like needles. The minister said that he wished to counsel us before he would marry us. Rick and I agreed to this. We went to see him a couple of times. My little cousins were going to be my flower girls, and another cousin made the dresses for them. Everything was coming together quite nicely. Brother Rob's wife, Ruth, was going to be my matron of honor, and my brother Rob was going to be the best man. I was now home again in Wichita, and the invitations were in. I got them and began sending them out. I tried one more time to get a hold of Dad, but Betty wouldn't allow it. I had no choice now but to send him an invitation to his work. When he got it, I just knew that he would want to be a part of my big day—a day that, a long time ago, we dreamed and talked about. My big day was coming closer, and still I got no word from my dad. My heart began to sink. I knew that he had gotten the invitation by then. Betty could not have intercepted it. Why didn't he respond? He surely knew that I needed him at my wedding. We talked about this and planned it years ago; surely, he just wouldn't ignore this and not show up. Who would walk me down the aisle if not my dad? It's days before my wedding, and still I received no word from my dad. I felt completely lost now; I didn't know what to do. My uncle Tom (my dad's brother) came to me and said that even though he was not my dad, he would consider it an honor if I would let him walk me down the aisle. I agreed and thanked him for offering to do so. Well, I was now ready for my wedding. I had my dress, Rick had a suit, and I had my flowers and garter. The cake was here, and everything was all set up for the reception. Everything looked great. I was well pleased. My day would not be the same without my dad, but I had to get through it. A part of me was still hoping that at the very last minute he would show up or at least be in the very back somewhere watching me—his little girl, his firstborn—get married. Once again, my father had disappointed me. I just couldn't believe he had turned on me this way.

Well, life must go on. The wedding was beautiful, and the reception was great. We received mostly money as a gift and spent our wedding night with family at the local bowling alley, of all places. Not at all what I dreamed my wedding night would be like. We didn't go on a honeymoon, because we didn't have the money to do so. After the bowling, we returned to my grandparents' house where we were staying the night. Rick wanted to consummate, and I said absolutely not because my grandma and granddad were in the room next to ours. He said they would understand and that they know what happens on wedding nights. I told him that I didn't care what they understand; I was not going to have sex with him while they were in the next room. It was just not going to happen. I told him that the next day was Sunday and they would go to church and then we could do it, but not until the next day. Well, the next day came, and my grandparents went to church, and we ended up breaking the bed. Actually, the bed was an old bed with the wooden slats supporting the box springs and mattress. The slats slipped out, and everything including us hit the floor with a very loud thud. This was exactly why I wouldn't do it the night before. If we had and this had happened then, I would have been so embarrassed and humiliated. I would have wanted to die; I would never have been able to face my grandparents again in life. Now my grandparents would never know that the bed fell apart. We did put it back together, and they were never the wiser. Well, after a couple of days, Rick and I headed for Wichita. Once there, we packed up all my things, rented a moving trailer, and moved to Denver, Colorado, where we lived and made our home. After arriving in Denver, we moved into a house with the same people I had originally went there to see to collect the car from. I never did get the car or any money, but I (we) lived with them rent-free. We all lived in an eight-bedroom rental house. They have four kids, plus themselves, and another renter, a single guy named Dexter. Rick and I settled in and enjoyed married life.

Since I was not working, I agreed to watch the two younger kids who were not in school. Everyone else in the house worked.

One day, about a month later, Rick didn't come home after work. No phone call, nothing. He didn't say anything that morning about being late that night or not coming home. I was worried but didn't know where to look, and I didn't have any transportation, because Rick had the car. Well, I went to bed thinking that he would be home by morning. Morning came, and he still wasn't home. The second day went by, and nighttime came and still no Rick. I was really worried. I didn't even know where to look for him. I went to bed on the second night crying myself to sleep.

Third day arrived, same thing, still no Rick. I called all the hospitals and nothing. I didn't know what to do. I was newly married, living in a strange city, hundreds of miles away from any family or real friends. The only people I knew were the ones I was living with, and I didn't know them all that well and had no transportation. I'd never been more alone and lost in my life. Days went by, and still no Rick and no word. I was beginning to think that I had been abandoned by my husband. Jack made some inquiries and found nothing. None of us knew what to do or even where to look. Two weeks went by, and the third week passed, and Christmas was approaching—my first Christmas as a married woman without a husband.

Christmas came and went without Rick. New Year's Eve was coming. I just went through my days in a daze then. I was just going through the motions of living. Everyone in the house tried to comfort me, but nothing helped. It's now New Year's Eve. At the stroke of midnight, I put on my coat and stepped out onto the back porch. I looked up to the heavens and asked for God's help. I knew that I hadn't talked to God in a long time and maybe he wouldn't even hear me, but I needed his help. I didn't know where else to turn. I asked God to give me a sign of some kind that would tell me everything would be all right. Then as sure as I was standing there and looking into the heavens, I saw a particular star got real super bright, as if to stand out from all the millions of others. Then it began to twinkle.

I took that as my sign from God that everything was going to be all right. Then, all of a sudden, this calming peace came over me. I knew in that moment that Rick would return, and everything would work itself out. A few days later, Jack came home and told me that he had located Rick. Rick was alive and well and sitting in jail in a town outside of Denver. Jack took me there to see him. I was so glad to see Rick. He was picked up on outstanding warrants and had been there all this time. He had no way of calling me since we didn't have a phone. I had never been more relieved in my life. Rick did not abandon me like I had thought. God was right. Everything was going to be all right, and I thanked him for that. Another two or three weeks went by before Rick was released from jail. Oh, what a happy day that was. I had my husband back. Life was good, and I was happy. We were being forced to move because they (Jack and Connie) could no longer afford the rent on the house. Rick said he had a friend that we could stay with until we find a place of our own. We ended up at this old run-down hotel in a not-so-good part of town. I was scared. This place was really bad. Rick said that he wouldn't let anything bad happen to me. The place was filthy, and it smelled bad. I had never seen anything like this place before. There were people sleeping on the floor in the hallways. You could hear yelling and screaming. There were fights going on. There were drunks and drug dealers and homeless people. There were cockroaches everywhere. *Oh my God, what have I gotten myself into? What has Rick gotten me into?* I thought. The room of the friend we were staying in was somewhat clean, cleaner than outside the room anyway. A person couldn't sleep at night because of all the racket and noise. We stay there for a couple of weeks before getting our own apartment in a nice security building way across town. The apartment building was a half block from the Capitol building, a much nicer place to live. Our apartment was a studio, small but very clean, and there were *no* bugs. We were on the second floor in the back of the building. After a few months, we moved to a vacated apartment on the third floor in the front of the building. I liked facing the street and watching out at everything. One day, Rick asked me why I was not on Social Security Disability. I didn't know anything about it. I thought it was for people who became disabled from wars, that you had to be a veteran from the military to get something like that. Rick said, no, you didn't and marched me right down to the Social Security Office. All the necessary paperwork was filled out. I was sent to a group of doctors and must parade around in front of them wearing a paper shirt and paper shorts. They needed to see that I didn't have an arm and that I have an artificial leg. A few weeks later, I received a letter of approval and, shortly thereafter, received a large back paycheck. We used the back paycheck to move back to Kansas. My mom was not well, and I wanted to be close to her. We moved to Fort Scott, Kansas, and there my Social Security checks began coming monthly. I was so glad to be home and near my family. Mom kept asking me when I was going to give her a grandchild. "When I get pregnant," I told her. Rick and I were not doing anything to prevent pregnancy. We were trying to conceive, but nothing was happening. As life went on, I noticed that Rick seemed to drink a lot. I guessed I really never noticed it before. He went to the local bars frequently after work. He stayed all evening there.

I didn't understand why he didn't come home and be with me. When I asked him about it, he just said that it had always been the way he was and I would have to deal with it. I didn't know how to deal with it. I knew what I could do—change him. I decided to make him into a good husband and then one day a good father.

My family had a lot of get-togethers for meals. Rick never wanted to attend any of them with me but always asked me to bring some food home for him. "I'll not do it," I told him. "If you want some food, then you could get off your butt and come with me," I told him. He said that he didn't like being around a bunch of people; it's just not his thing, he said. Well, I was a people person, and I love my family very much, so I went and always had a good time. My family always asked about Rick, and I just told them that he didn't want to come. I thought, *Oh, well, it's his loss.*

Time went by, and I finally went to see a doctor to see why I was not getting pregnant. I seemed to check out just fine. The doctor then asked Rick for a sample of his sperm. A sperm count was run, and Rick's sperm count was very low. Minor surgery had to be done to correct the problem. The doctor said that it would take about three months for his sperm count to return to normal after the surgery. I lost my grandma in the summer of 1982. What a loss. I didn't know how our family would survive this.

Grandma was like the backbone of the family. Now we all worried about Granddad. I worried how he would survive without her. She took care of him. Hell, she took care of everyone. They were married for forty-nine years. I asked myself, what was going to happen to this family?

None of us could imagine life without Grandma. Rick and I decided that it was a good time for him to have the surgery. So the surgery went off without a hitch. I told Mom that when he is healed and his sperm count goes back up to normal, then I would hopefully get pregnant. Mom was what the doctors called an "out-of-control" diabetic. When her pancreas was removed a few years earlier, the doctors were unable to get her insulin regulated, so she was constantly going into those diabetic comas. We most generally could bring her out of them with sweetened orange juice. Occasionally, we would have to call an ambulance to take her to the hospital; they could always bring her around. She was suffering physically more and more every day. She said that her joints ached constantly. She had lost so much weight, but she ate all the time. She looked like a skeleton with skin hanging on it. She carried around a pillow to sit on because she had no meat on her butt, so most chairs that she sat on were too hard for her. Rick and I only lived about a block and a half from my mom. On September 27, 1982, Mom and I went shopping and had lunch. She said for the first time in months and months, she was without any pain, and she looked great. She hadn't looked this good since I couldn't remember when. I could tell she had no pain. She was laughing, and we were having such a great time, a mother-and-daughter day. We got home about 1:30 or 2:00. She said she was a little tired and was going to lie down and take a little nap before David got home from school. David came down to my house around 4:00 or 4:30 and said Mom was in another one of her comas and he couldn't wake her up. I told him that I would be there in a few minutes. I had been napping also and had to get up and get dressed. When I arrived at the house, my granddad, who lived next door, was with her, as well as David.

Granddad kept saying, "I think she's gone, Diana." I told him that we've been through this many times before and that she would be just fine. An ambulance had been called and was on its way. I told Granddad to ride with her in the ambulance to the hospital and that I would be along shortly. I went back up to my house because I had walked to Mom's. I told Rick what was going on, and he drove us to the hospital. When we walked into the emergency room and I looked at Granddad, he looked back at me, shaking his head, and said that she was gone. In that moment, everything around me went white, and I collapsed. I came to a short while later on a gurney in an emergency room cubicle. I demanded to see my mother. I was told that she had died. I didn't care, I said, I needed to see her; and so they took me to see her body. I thought, what was I going to do without my mom? I had lost both my grandma and my mom within a few months of each other. That night, Rick and I had sex. He said it would help take my mind off things for a while, and then a few hours later, I got really sick. The next few days, I was walking around in a fog. Aunt Betty helped Rob and I plan Mothers' funeral. We'd never done anything like that before and didn't know what to do. Aunt Betty was a great help. She walked us through every step. Mother was a very simple woman, and so her funeral was also simple, and I thought she would have approved. A few weeks went by since Mom died, and I find out that I was pregnant. Well, I realized two things: (1) God never took a life without giving you another, and (2) I know now that I got pregnant the night Mom died. I wished Mom could be there. Aunt Betty really stepped up to help and offer any advice that I might have needed or wanted. I was thrilled about having a baby. My pregnancy went very well; there was no morning sickness. I felt great all the way along. At seven months along, Rick took off and said he had to go and find work elsewhere because we lived in a small town and he couldn't get a decent-paying job to support our family. He wouldn't tell me where he was going; he said that if anybody came looking for him, I wouldn't be lying when I said that I didn't know where he was. I asked him who was going to be looking for him. He said no one that he knew of, but just in case. I didn't understand what the secrecy was all about, and he refused to tell me. When I asked him what about when I went into labor, he said he would be back in time for the birth. I was due at the end of June. He said that after the baby is born, we would all move to where he was working, wherever that is. A week or so after he was gone, the police came to my home asking for Rick. I told them the truth, that I didn't know where he was. I asked what this was about, and they said that they can't tell me. I had absolutely no idea what he had done and was scared to really know. While he was gone and I was in my eighth month of pregnancy, I ended up having to move from the house where we were to a more affordable apartment. Right at that moment, the only money I had was my disability checks, and he hadn't sent me any money, so I couldn't afford the house. Some friends helped me pack and move.

It was my ninth month, and I had to unpack and set up house and get ready for the birth of my baby. Rick didn't call very often. He did know that I had to move. When he called me, he said he felt really sorry about it when he found out. In the second week of June, I sort of sprung a leak. Some women say their water broke. Mine didn't break; it sprung a leak. It started out just a little. I woke up at night and thought I had wet the bed. I changed myself and the bed and went back to sleep. Next morning, I was wet again. During the day, I kept leaking to the point that I started wearing a sanitary pad to catch it.

By the second day, I had a hand towel between my legs. Having never been pregnant before, I didn't know what was normal. By the third day, Saturday, the eleventh of June, I had to sit with a folded bath towel. My friend Carolyn came and took me to the emergency room. They admitted me and told me that I was not going back home. I told them that I was not in labor. They said that they were going to induce my labor. I told them that I couldn't have the baby yet because the dad was not there and didn't even know that I was there. They said that it would take several hours, so he should have plenty of time to get there. I didn't even know where he was to call him. My aunt Betty and uncle Tom came to the hospital along with some of my cousins and of course my friend Carolyn. While in the labor room and having *no* pains, there was a fifteen-year-old girl across the hall in the delivery room having her baby and screaming to the top of her lungs. Then there was a woman in the cubicle next to me in labor with her third child and getting pretty loud. I was getting a little scared now. I had no idea what labor was going to feel like, but I was hearing it all around me, and I didn't think I want to do this anymore, and I was alone with no husband or mom. The hospital induced my labor, and my first contraction hit at 11:00 p.m. Oh my God, the pain was so intense. I changed my mind, decided I didn't want to do it, but I knew there was no turning back, so I did not make a sound, and I would not scream. I thought I would endure it as I had endured everything else that I had been thru.

Having this baby was my choice; it was a planned pregnancy. By this time tomorrow, it would all be over and my baby boy would be here and somehow so would Rick. I just knew I was having a boy because the doctor said by the heartbeat it was a boy, and family members said I was carrying the baby low, which was also a sign that it was a boy. Right then, the pain was unreal. I had a death grip on the bed rail. I was panting like a dog; it's helping. With induction of labor, you go straight into hard labor, and I did mean *hard*. Exactly sixty-nine minutes from the first contraction at 11:00 p.m., my baby was born. It's 12:09 a.m. on June 12, 1983, when the doctor said to me that he would like to introduce my little girl to her mother. "Yeah, right," I said, "let me see my son." Doc said, "Really, you have a baby girl. See, look at her." I was momentarily in shock. I believed all this time (months) that I was carrying a boy. I look at the baby; it really was a girl. I said to myself, "Okay, now that I have a daughter, I have to completely shift my thinking." After she was cleaned up and weighed and everything else that they do to newborns, she was brought to me in recovery. The first thing that I did was unwrap the blanket that she's in and strip her clothes off. I looked and investigated and counted every finger and toe. I even turn her over to see her backside. I wanted to look at and memorize every inch of this most beautiful creature. She was the most beautiful and precious thing I had ever seen. I was absolutely overwhelmed with emotions. I had never felt this kind of love before for anyone or anything. It was an all-consuming would-absolutely-die-for-to-protect kind of love. *Wow*, was all I could think of when I looked at her. I wished Mom could be there and meet and hold her granddaughter. I knew then that Mom had to go in order for me to have my daughter. The next day, there was still no sign of Rick, or the next or the next. I spent a week in the hospital with no sign of Rick. He didn't even know I had had our baby. He didn't know that he had a daughter. Aunt Betty bought an outfit for my daughter (Kalena Elizabeth) to wear home from the hospital. After I got home, some family members, cousins, and such came by to see me and the baby. After a few hours, everyone was gone, and I was alone with my daughter. This was not at all what I envisioned my life to be like with child. I thought, *Where is Rick, and why hasn't he called?* My mind went places that I didn't want to think about. After about two weeks, Rick finally called, and I told him the news that we have a beautiful baby girl. He was very surprised. I asked when he was coming home, and he said it would be soon. I felt so alone. I didn't have a mother anymore and was estranged from my dad and had been for several years, and my husband was not there, either. I did call my dad and tell him that he had a new baby granddaughter. He asked all the usual questions that one asked about a new baby. He congratulated me, and the call ended. He didn't ask to see her or for a picture. I had lived with so much disappointment in my life, and this was just another one. I had spoken with my in-laws, whom I had never met but wrote to and talked to on the phone occasionally. Rick finally gave in and reached out to them a year ago or so. They knew all about me, but we had never met. They were Frank and Ruby, and they lived near Milwaukee, Wisconsin, and were thrilled to have another grandchild. Sometime in August, Rick finally came back, and all he wanted to do was have sex. He never seemed to be satisfied where that was concerned. I, on the other hand, could do without it. In fact, I hated it. We fought and argued all the time about that subject. He said that there was something very wrong with me to hate sex like I do. He was probably right, but I was too embarrassed to seek any help, and we didn't have the money anyway. I just went thru the motions whenever we had sex. Rick always asked me, "Did you get off'?" When I said no, he then said, "Oh, well, I did," and that was all that matters. I just did my wifely duty and went on. I always thought that sex was supposed to be this wonderful experience, but it's not for me. I guessed this was just another part of life that I had to live and deal with.

In September, my in-laws came for a visit. I was excited to meet them and to introduce their granddaughter to them. Mom (Ruby) watched everything I did with and for Kalena. I knew she just wanted to see how I took care of her with only one arm. She watched me feed and burp her, and change her diaper and clothes. She watched me bathe her, and even how I picked her up and lay her down. At the end of the week, when they were getting ready to head back home, Mom (Ruby) told me that after having watched how I cared for Kalena, she'd never worry about her being cared for by me again. She had told me that before they got here, she had wondered how I did things with one arm. She said that I not only fascinated her, but I also put her mind at ease. Rick's parents also invited us to come to Wisconsin to live. They said that we could live with them until we could get our own place. Milwaukee, being a big city, had more opportunity for work than little Fort Scott, Kansas, could offer. We took them up on their offer, and the first of October 1983, we packed up everything we owned and moved up to Wisconsin. I looked at this as an adventure. I'd never been there before and was looking forward to the change. *Maybe this is where my destiny lies,* I thought. I just couldn't help but know and feel that I was destined for more than just this kind of life. I just didn't know what it was that I was supposed to do or where I was supposed to go. I didn't even know how to find this out.

Whenever I mentioned anything to Rick about it, he just said that I was a dreamer, to just get over it, that this was my life and I had to deal with it. A couple of days after arriving in Wisconsin, Rick went out and got drunk and totaled our car, our only transportation. Rick didn't socialize much with my family, and he didn't socialize much with his family either. A couple of weeks later, I got a phone call from Aunt Betty telling me that my other grandma (Cooper), my dad's mom, passed away. I was unable to get back for the funeral, so my mother-in-law helped me to send flowers. The holidays came, and Rick didn't even join in with the festivities. Mom (Ruby) made him go out and do Christmas shopping to get me something. On Christmas Day, he was very antisocial. Gifts were exchanged, and we were getting ready to go over to his sister's house for Christmas dinner when out of the blue he announced to me in front of his parents that he had an affair with someone back in Fort Scott. Well, Merry Christmas to me. I was horrified and humiliated. I had never been more embarrassed in my entire life. I somehow knew that this was true. I suspected as much at the time but didn't want to believe it; but to be told on of all days, Christmas, and in front of his parents, this was a very personal jab at me. I must put on a happy face for my daughter and go with his folks to Brenda and Bob's (Rick's sister and brother-inlaw) home for dinner. I was sure that Mom told Brenda and Bob what happened back at the house. I just pretended like nothing was wrong, but what I really wanted to do was to crawl into a very deep dark hole and never come out. I thought it just couldn't be my life; but I knew I must somehow go on for my daughters' sake; I just didn't yet know how. I had, however, told Rick that sometime after the first of the year when I had enough money saved up for airline tickets, I was taking my daughter and going back to Kansas without him. Well, a new year had arrived, and I could only hope that this year would be a whole new beginning for me. Brenda called me and said that she and Bob would like to take me out on the town before I leave and show me some of Milwaukee. They took me out for dinner to a place where a reservation and tie were required—I had never been anywhere like that—and then to another place for drinks that rotated on top of a huge building. I had the time of my life and so appreciated the time out, since I rarely left the house once I got to Wisconsin in October.

I had made arrangements for Kalena and me to stay at my granddad's house in Fort Scott. Aunt Betty and Uncle Tom picked us up at the Kansas City airport. I was sort of glad to be back home again in Kansas. I thought I must figure out what to do next. The first thing was that I needed a car, some form of transportation. A few weeks later, Uncle Tom helped me find a real good used car, which I bought. Living with my granddad was really great. I was seeing him in a way that I never had before. He was a very kind and gentle man. He was also from the old school, though, and very old-fashioned and set in his ways. I had learned that those ways really weren't so bad after all. He taught my daughter how to get down off the couch. She kept trying to go head first, but he kept turning her around and turning her around until she finally got the hang of going feetfirst. It was so cool watching him with her; he had so much patience with her. Granddad was such a big man, and when he held Kalena, she looked so small in his arms. He and grandma always had this brown crock cookie jar that was always full of cookies, and he still keeps it that way. Kalena had learned about that cookie jar, and she knew exactly where it's at. After a couple of months more, I had saved enough money to get us an apartment. Aunt Betty, Uncle Tom, Granddad, and some other family members provided me with enough furnishings to set up house since all my things were still in Wisconsin. I had to borrow literally everything, a bed, bedding, a crib and crib bedding, towels and washcloths, dishes, pots and pans, a couch and a chair, an end table, and a lamp. Once I got settled into my new apartment, I then must save up enough money to begin divorce proceedings. During this time, I learned that my brother Joe was getting married, and I was invited to the wedding. I travelled to Fall River, Kansas, with my daughter to Joe's wedding, hoping maybe to see my dad, thinking Joe had invited him. I hoped that if Dad could be there, he didn't bring Betty. If he could be there, then he'd get to see his granddaughter for the first time. She was eleven months old then. If he would hold her, I would like to get a picture of them, because after that day I didn't know when I would see him again or when he would see his granddaughter again, so I just gotta get a picture. Upon arrival, I saw that dad was there and without Betty but had David with him. David looked real good and healthy. Kim was also there; wow, she's all grown up and looked so beautiful. I got a picture of Dad holding Kalena, with David, and another picture later of Kim and Kalena. At this wedding, I met for the first time the girl my brother was marrying. She was extremely young. I didn't see this marriage lasting, but I hoped for the best. After a while, they moved to Fort Scott and into Granddad's house. They stayed there for a while, then moved into a place of their own. I didn't like this girl at all. She was nothing more than a child who couldn't cook or clean. Joe came to me one day and asked me to try to teach her how to cook. Yeah right, I didn't even like her, and he wanted me to be around her and teach her to cook. I tried, but she really didn't seem interested in learning. Joe went to work and then came home and had to cook and clean. She went to Granddad's house and called her family long distance on his phone and ran up his bill. Granddad told me that some things were missing from his house. I went over to her and Joe's apartment and found the things that were missing from granddad's house and just went off on her.

She started to walk away from me, and I grabbed her arm and swung her around and then slapped her across the face. Joe then grabbed my arm and told me not to hit his wife, and I told him that she had been stealing from Granddad and that if he didn't remove his hand off my arm I would hit him too. He let go of my arm. She then ran into the bedroom and yelled that she would go home to her mama. I yelled back at her that that was exactly what a child would do—run home to mama. She changed her mind after that. Joe decided awhile later that he would enlist in the navy. He sent her home to live with her mother while he was away. I never saw her again.

Rick had contacted me and wanted to get back together. He told me that he was very sorry and that he didn't want a divorce and begged for a second chance. I felt for our daughter's sake that I had to try and make this marriage work, so I agreed to let him come back to me. He moved back to Fort Scott and into my apartment. He had a broken arm and said that he was hit by a lady who ran a red light. He said that there were witnesses and that everything was turned into her insurance company and a settlement would be coming when all was settled. Rick got a job working second shift at a local factory. All went well for us, and then we decided to find a house to rent. We ended up moving to small town a few miles north of Fort Scott called Prescott, Kansas. The house was really very old and not very well insulated but nice. The landlords were an elderly couple that live right next door. Rick decided one day that we needed a dog, so he found this little puppy and brought it home. The puppy looked like a little bear cub, so that was what his name became, Bear. A few weeks later, the puppy died from a puppy disease called parvo. Rick had met and become fast friends with a guy he worked with named Mike. Mike had a live-in girlfriend named Tina. She and I meet and became good friends. Mike's parents raised, bred, and sold Doberman pinschers. Rick wanted one and asked me about it. I told him that they were a dangerous breed and that they could turn on you. I was thinking of my daughter's safety. I didn't want one to turn on her and eat her. He said that if they were raised from a puppy with love and care, they would be all right. I finally agreed but insisted on a female and a black-and-tan one. We went to Mike's parents place and picked one out, a beautiful twelve-week-old black-and-tan female that we had to pay fifty dollars for. We called her Lady because of her markings. I had never had a dog that I actually had to buy, and that was a purebred and with papers too. I took her to the vet and got all the necessary shots, definitely didn't want this one dying on me. I found out that ears had to be surgically cut in order for her to stand up, so I got that done also. For the next several weeks, we had to change the bandages on her ears. Kalena absolutely loved this dog. She wallers all over the dog, and even tried to ride her. The dog had even grown very fond of Kalena. This was exactly what I wanted for both of them.

They were becoming inseparable. Lady learned commands very quickly and minded very well. She was extremely smart and very loving. I had fallen in love with her. I was also the disciplinarian in the household with the dog and the kid. Rick just played with them and left the rest to me. Rick had a very, very foul mouth. Every other word out of his mouth was the *f* word. It's always f——k that or f——k this or just f——k, f——k, f——k. I had also picked up this colorful language. After a while, I didn't even realize that I was saying it myself. We're both cigarette smokers, and having been introduced to marijuana by Rick, we both were pot smokers too. Rick drank beer a lot, but I was not a drinker except for my coffee and sweet iced tea.

Kalena liked coffee too. Hers had more milk than coffee, but she didn't know the difference. I thought I shouldn't have been so shocked when Kalena's first cuss word was the *f* word, but I sure was. Rick had left to go visit with Mike. After he left, she climbed up on my lap and asked me where her daddy went. When I told her that he went to Mike's house, she said, "Well, f——k." I almost died when she said that word. I tried to explain that that was a bad word and that mommy and daddy should not say it and that she could never say it again. When I told Rick, he thought it was funny. I told Rick that we had to really watch what we say because of her, but he said she would learn it in the world anyway, and he refused to quit saying it. At least, she didn't have to know the words *pot* and *marijuana*, because we never said those words. We referred to that stuff as "smoke," so if we were in public and she were to say Mommy and Daddy smoke, no one would think twice since both of us smoke cigarettes. I was convinced that "pot" wouldn't hurt you or damage you in any way, and besides, I liked it and enjoyed smoking it. The settlement from Rick's accident finally came in, and it was for about $12,500 after attorney fees. We got a second car, "a local bank repo," and then went shopping for new beds, waterbeds in fact, for us and Kalena. We did a lot of shopping for all kinds of things and paid a couple of bills. Rick then told me that he and Mike were going to buy a large quantity of "pot" and sell it and make a lot of money. I was not at all crazy about that idea. Smoking it was one thing, but dealing it was another. All of it was illegal, but to be selling it really bothered me, but he said he's doing it anyway. I told him that I would not lose my daughter over some stupid weed, and he said that I wouldn't.

This old house that we rented had strange things that happened that we couldn't explain. I believed that everything could be explained somehow someway. There were times that we couldn't always afford disposable diapers, so we used cloth diapers and plastic pants on Kalena. I had a diaper pail in the bathroom for the dirty cloth diapers to be put in. Occasionally, I found a diaper on the floor in the bathroom first thing in the morning. Knowing that I didn't put it there in the middle of the night, I asked Rick why he didn't put it into the pail. He swore that he didn't change her diaper in the middle of the night. So how and why was the diaper on the floor? The furnace got turned up as high as it would go during the night. I didn't do it, Rick swore he didn't do it, Kalena couldn't have done it, so how did it happen?

Kalena's bottles got removed from the refrigerator in the middle of the night. I didn't do it, again Rick swore that he didn't do it, and no one else could have done it. So again how were these things happening? Food was also vanishing from the fridge without any explanation. Rick and I couldn't figure any of this out at all. We decided that maybe the house might be haunted since it was so old, but we were not sure if we believe in any of that stuff. Occasionally, even the dog acted like there was something in the house that couldn't be seen by us. She seemed to sense something there and even growled at we didn't know what. We didn't seem to feel afraid of whatever it might have been. I thought that as long as we didn't feel afraid or "it" didn't hurt my child, whatever "it" was, we'd be all right. We ended up living in this house for about a year before moving to our next place. We moved across the state line into Missouri. The house we ended up renting was larger and nicer than the one we just left. It had three bedrooms, and right away, Rick decided to turn one of the bedrooms into a growing room for marijuana plants. He put cardboard over the windows, then covered them with aluminum foil. He ordered a huge halloid (growing light) and hung it from the ceiling to provide proper lighting for the growing of the plants. Right across the street from our house were railroad tracks. The train came through several times a day and night, and the house just rumbled. After a while, we got used to the train.

The only time it's annoying was when we were on the phone or watching TV, and then we just had to wait for it to pass before continuing a conversation on the phone. If we're watching TV, the volume got turned up real loud till the train passed. Our dog Lady had really taken to Kalena, and she to the dog. They both were very protective of each other. Lady literally slept in the bed with Kalena, and Kalena wouldn't go to bed without the dog. It was really cute to see those two together. The pot plants were coming along nicely and really getting to be a nice size. Rick and Mike's little project was doing well. Then one night, out of the blue, Mike showed up and said that he heard that the police had been monitoring a house in the town where we lived and that it was about to be raided. So not knowing if our house was the one, I told the two of them to get those plants out of my house that very night.

When they asked where to take them, I said I didn't really care what they did with them and to just get rid of them from my house. I insisted they tear down the cardboard, tin foil; everything in that room had to go that night. Then we put a bunch of junk in the room to make it look like a catchall room or junk room. We never saw hide nor hair of any police that night or any other night. Rick and Mike were really pissed off at me for making them get rid of the plants. Oh, well, too bad. Rick should've been mad at Mike for telling us about the police possibly watching our house, but nooooo. I learned later that Rick and Mike had replanted the plants down by some river somewhere. Those two would come up with some of the most outrageous schemes to make money, all the while working at day jobs. Rick would set up late at night watching all those get-rich-quick infomercials. He spent more money on those than you could believe. Then his best friend Steve called and wanted Rick to go over the road on the big rig with him. Steve would pay him to work for him, so Rick agreed and left. I was fine with the plan. Every other week or so, Rick would send me money. Not much money but some. My Social Security disability paid the rent and most of the bills. After Rick was gone awhile, I decided that I really didn't want him to come back, so after informing him of that, I decided to move again to another small town ten miles down the road to a small house and cheaper rent that was easier for me to afford on my own. The town I moved to was called Butler Missouri. There I made a home for my daughter and myself. The house was small but just right for Kalena and me. The first morning in our new place was stressful. I had no groceries in the house and no cash on hand, but I had my Social Security check and my daughter's check. I went to a local bank in town and asked them to cash one of the checks, but they refused because I didn't have an account with them. I said that they could charge me so much if they would just cash the smaller of the two checks. Again, they refused.

I left there and went to another local bank and tried again. By then, my daughter, who was three years old, was crying and hungry. The second bank told me the same thing. I didn't have an account; therefore, they couldn't help me. I absolutely couldn't believe this. I had about $900 in two checks and all the identification they need, but because I didn't have an account with them, they wouldn't help me. As a mother, I was so frustrated. I wanted to feed my hungry crying child, and I couldn't. I went to yet another bank, the third one, Bates County National Bank. I asked them to cash just one of my government checks, the smaller one in fact. I showed them all of the identification I had, and they told me that they would have to charge me a few dollars, but that they could do it with no problems. Because they helped me out when no one else would, I gave them my business and opened an account with them and was proud to do so. Now I could feed my hungry child and buy groceries. That was such a wonderful feeling. I knew then that we were going to be just fine—she and I and Lady, our dog. We were all the family we need, Kalena and I together against the world. Kalena and I both have waterbeds, and I had become quite good at putting them together by myself. They were almost like putting a puzzle together. The only help I needed was lifting the headboard on my bed as I had a king-size bed. Now I began the task of unpacking things and finding a place for everything. I hated unpacking boxes as much as I hated packing them. You would think that I would stay in one place for a really long time, but I didn't. I seemed to have moved about once a year since I moved away from home. Kalena and I settled into our new place. I got her room all set up and organized, so she had a place to sleep and play and hopefully feel comfortable. This house was very small, but for just the two of us, it would do for that moment. Kalena and I watched our favorite game show every morning. We loved the *Price Is Right* with Bob Barker. The way she said his name was so cute, and when someone's name was called, Kalena said, "Come on down." Kalena said that when she grew up, she wanted to go to play that game and meet Bob Barker. We also listened to music every day, country music in fact. Alabama was our most favorite singing group. Kalena loved them so much. She got one of her Lego pieces and used it as a microphone; then she climbed up on top of her toy box, which became her stage and just sang along with the music. I wished I had a camera. She said that when she grows up, she is going to tour and sing with Alabama. I always told her that she could do anything she wanted to. She always said back to me, "I would, Mama." I love this child more than words can say. She may never know the depths of my love for her. The washer and dryer hookup was in my bedroom, and the floor was concrete with carpet only on half the floor. There were a lot of trees around this house, and I thought that tree roots had gotten into the drainpipes around the house. All the drains in this place were very slow. Whenever I did, the laundry the drained back up. Water backed up into the tub and sink. I contacted the landlord, and he sent his maintenance man over with a plunger and some drain cleaner. I could not believe this. I told the man that he was going to need more than that to fix this problem. He said the owner/landlord was real cheap and wouldn't fork out the money. "Oh yes, he will," I told him. My waterbed had upward of a thousand gallons of water in it, and if the water in my room from the backed-up drain caused the wood to warp or rot on my bed and break, it would have flooded this house and ruined everything I owned and I would have sued him so fast he wouldn't know what hit him. The landlord heard about this and contacted a Roto-Rooter guy to clear the drain lines and then complained to me that the guy charged him $100 to clear the lines. I told him that that was far less than what he would have had to pay out if my bed had gotten ruined and broke. He agreed. The maintenance guy Chuck was pretty cool. He had a nice family, a wife and two sons. We became friends. He told me that nobody had ever spoken to the owner/landlord the way I did and got away with it. Chuck said anybody else would have gotten an eviction notice. Chuck said the man was not nice at all and was basically a slumlord. Well, Kalena and I settled into our place and were doing okay. One day, out of the blue, there's a knock at the door.

When I opened the door, there stood Rick. *How did he find us? What does he want?* Those were the questions running through my mind. We didn't need him. He asked to come in and talk. Kalena was happy to see her dad, and he her. He begged me to let him come back, said he was sorry for everything, and would do his best to change and be better. For Kalena's sake, I agreed. I really didn't want a divorce and be another statistic in the world. A few months later, while at the city park, Rick and I noticed a house across from the park that appeared to be empty. We went and checked it out. There's no for-sale or -rent sign anywhere. There was a paper in the garage-door window that said something about being property of the US government. It's a real nice raised ranch house on a corner lot, appeared to have three bedrooms, and attached garage with full basement. While looking in the windows, we saw a very clean and beautiful home. We wondered how and why it belonged to the government. Could it have been seized in a drug bust or what? Over the next few weeks, we asked around about the house and learned that the house was owned by Farmers Home Administration. They had housing for low-income families. There were eight of the houses, five on that street with the one that we want on the corner and three more on the street behind. Upon further investigation, we learned how to apply for the house and do so. I'd never seen so much paperwork in my life. After we got everything filled out and sent in, we waited. Rick was working at a local ladder factory and making a decent wage, and with my Social Security check, we did okay. All of our bills were paid and current, so we didn't see any problems against us in getting the house. Our only concern was that we were told that, although there would not be a down payment like buying from a bank, we had to pay all closing costs. That consisted of the first month's mortgage payment, proof of first year of insurance, and the closing fees. We were told that it would total about $1,000. We didn't have that kind of money, and I didn't know where we would get it. *Oh, well,* I thought, *I shouldn't be worrying about that at the moment, not until I find out if we have even been approved. If we get the house, we'd breed and raise Doberman puppies to sell as a sideline income.* A few months later, we received notice that we had been approved to get the house. I was so very excited.

We were going to be homeowners. Wow, I couldn't wait to get moved, but, first, we had to find the closing costs money. Rick called his parents and told them the situation, and they sent us the money.

I couldn't believe that they would do this for us, but they did. We got moved into our own home two weeks after Kalena's fourth birthday. It's a beautiful home and was only two years old, with one previous owner who only lived in it for a year. The property didn't have any trees or shrubbery anywhere. There wasn't and any kind of air conditioner either. We soon discovered that with no trees to help shade the house and no air conditioner and it being a raised ranch-style home, it got very, very hot inside. I thought, *Maybe next year we could afford an air conditioner, but not this year. We'll have to suffer through this somehow.* Kalena loved living across the street from the park. She wanted to go there every day. She's just not old enough to go over there by herself. Besides, we had a lot of unpacking to do and things to get put away to make our house a home. We had fans blowing everywhere to try and keep somewhat cool, but that was next to impossible in the heat of the summer. Our house was all electric. We had two electric meters on the side of the house. At some point, I was thinking that the electric bill should level out so that we would know what the average bill should be. So far, the bill had went up every single month that we'd been there. I was beginning to think that we were paying for the park lights to be on at night. I even started reading the meter myself and still could not understand why the bill just kept going up. I brought this to the attention of the electric company. They came out and tested our meters and the transformer. The bill continued to go up every month. I still complained to the electric company. Then they came out and changed the transformer and replaced the meters on my house.

They said that they didn't understand it either. I had proof that the bill had gone up every month since we took possession of the house, and the city couldn't seem to explain it either. Now winter was coming and our furnace was electric, I wondered what that was going to do to the bill. We couldn't have been able to keep up with these electric bills at this rate. I finally got fed up with these bills and threatened the electric company and the city with a ten-million-dollar lawsuit. All of a sudden, for the next several months, the bill dropped steadily. Go figure. How did the threat of a lawsuit cause the electric bill to steadily drop? Again, I got no answers but was glad that the bills started coming down. Rick turned back to his drinking again. He quit his job, and then we were just getting by on my Social Security. He stayed up all night watching TV or going to the local bars until they closed and then slept all day. We were fighting all the time because of his drinking. I didn't know where he was getting the money to drink, though. He said it's my fault that he drank. I told him that if he was that unhappy, then he should leave. He said that he wasn't going anywhere, because that it was his house, too, and that I couldn't afford it on my own. That's when I reminded him that I was paying for everything because he was not working. He's still said that he ain't leaving. My friend said that I didn't understand Rick's drinking because I am not a drinker myself. No, I didn't get it. He went out and got drunk, then came home and wanted to have sex. Really? Then when he couldn't do anything because of being so drunk, it's my fault somehow. I absolutely couldn't stand to have sex with him. I told him that if I never have sex again in life, it truly wouldn't bother me. He said that that's not normal for any woman. "Who wants to have sex with a drunk?" I asked. Then he again blamed me for his drinking. He found a place in Kansas City that took people for medical research. They paid you to stay there anywhere from a few days to a few weeks. So he contacted them, and he was accepted. I took him up there, and he was at this facility for about a month and then came home with $900. He also did odd jobs for different people for cash. I never saw much, if any, of the money. He continued to drink. Sometimes, I didn't see him for days. I prayed to God to just let him die. We only had one car, and he took it, leaving me stranded with nothing. How dare he. I truly hated this man. Whenever he did come home, he was usually drunk. I asked him if he had a girlfriend. I prayed he'd say yes and that he'd be leaving me for her. He told me no and that he just liked to get drunk and that he just passed out in the car. All I could say was, "Whatever." He finally got another job working at a moving company up toward Kansas City. Since we only had the one car, I told him that he was not leaving me stranded without the car anymore. So I got up early every morning with Kalena and drove him to the job an hour away and back. I then drove back up there in the evening to pick him up and come home again. I started hiding the keys to the car so that he couldn't take it anymore. He got really mad, but I had no fear of him hitting me. We had that discussion once a long time ago. I told him that if he ever lay so much as a finger on me, I would go into court in a wheelchair without my leg on and play the part of a poor defenseless crippled woman, and he being a big man of about 225 pounds beat me up. I would milk my disability for all it was worth, and the judge would put him in jail and probably throw away the key. He asked if I'd really do that, and I said, "Hell yes, I would. Just try me." That's how I knew he would never hit me. He did, however, use verbal abuse. Why I took even that, I didn't know. He called me everything but a white woman when he was mad at me. The only time he ever got really mad was when he drank. When he was sober, he was a great guy. He truly had a heart of gold and would give any stranger the shirt off his back. One day, he asked me about my dad. "What do you want to know?" I asked him. He asked me if I were truly in trouble whether my dad would help me. I told him no. He said that surely he would help his granddaughter. Again, I told him no. He then told me that he didn't believe me. Now I had to prove to Rick that my dad wouldn't help me or Kalena. Rick said for me to call my dad and tell him that he was kicking us out of the house and that we have nowhere to go and ask him if we could stay with him just for a short time until I could get on my feet. Since we had two phones in the house, Rick listened in on the extension while I was on the other phone talking to my dad. I told him the situation and asked him for help. He said he had to ask Betty, and then a minute or so later, he came back and told me, "You made your bed. Now you lay in it," and hung up on me. Rick was in shock that my dad would turn away from his own granddaughter. "I told you so," I said. My dad was not the dad I knew; he's not the dad he used to be. I didn't know him anymore. I know that this was all Betty's doing. I believed that if it were strictly up to Dad, he would take us in, at least temporarily anyway. My youngest brother, David, called me out of the blue and said that he needed a place to stay. He told me that he no longer lived with Dad and Betty. He was currently staying at brother Rob but that Rob said he had to get out. So I told him that he could come here and stay for a short while. There would be rules in which he must abide by, and he said okay and would be on his way. Oh my, I hadn't been around my brother in several years, and I thought it would become very interesting. Rick said that David would have a couple of weeks to find a job. I agreed with that. He was eighteen years old and was not just going to live off us. The only thing was that David didn't have a car, so we would have to be his transportation for a while. We had to get him to and from his job, depending on where it was, at least until he could make some friends and or get a car.

This was a small town, and there weren't any taxis or buses around here. When he finally did get here, I realized he had grown so much since the last time I saw him. He's all grown up then, and no longer that little boy that I remembered. I hadn't seen him since Mother died, and he went back to live with Dad and Betty; it had been six years.

He had gotten so tall, over six feet, I think. He looked good, though, healthy. I was really glad to see him; it's going to be nice to catch up. I believed that Mother would have been proud of David and how he had grown up. Well, within the first week David did get a job, and it's up north toward Kansas City, and there was a bus that took the workers there, but he had to be at our local store parking lot to catch that bus at like 5:00 or 5:30 in the morning. Well, since he did have a job, one of us, Rick or I, took him every morning to catch that bus. When David started getting a paycheck, we insisted that he give us so much out of it for food, which he did so willingly. Since he was there living with us, Rick and I took advantage of having a babysitter and asked him to stay with Kalena while we went out one night, and he agreed. Later when we came home, we found out that he got angry with Kalena and put a dog leash around her neck and chained her to a doorknob. I became outraged, and so did Rick. Who did he think he was to do that to a little girl? I could just beat him to death for that. We yelled at him for a long time over that. Three months later, Rick and I went out again and asked David if he could watch Kalena. He said yes, and we gave strict instructions about her—no more chaining her to doors. "If you get angry with her, then just send her to her room," we told him. This time, when we came home, he locked her inside a kitchen cabinet. She liked to play in my cabinets, and I allowed her to do that. David said when she crawled into one, he shut it and either sat against the doors or put something against them so she could not get out. He really thought it was funny. We again saw no humor in it. After jumping his ass for that, we never left her with him ever again. I noticed that David picked on Kalena constantly. I was always getting onto him about it, telling him to leave her alone.

She was only, like, five years old, and he was eighteen. After a few months, Rick and I decided that David had to find somewhere else to live. Before we could tell him that, he came and told us that he was going to be moving on. We all agreed that it's the best for everyone. I wished him well and told him that I loved him, and off he went into the world with a friend who came to pick him up. Rick did not care too much for black people, never had. He had always told me that he was not prejudiced against black people, that he thought everyone should own at least one. I didn't think that was funny at all. I had never had any problems with anyone of color. One day, while he was at work, Kalena was playing at the park with a neighbor boy her age named Matthew. They played together at the park all the time. She came and asked if she could go to his house and play. He lived up the street from us about five houses down. My rule always was that she could play outside only, and I said yes. Pretty soon, she came and told me that Matthew had asked her to go inside and play, and again my rule was not until I meet and get to know the parents. So then she asked me to meet his mom. Her name was Carmen, she said. Kalena said Mom Carmen was a nice lady. So I then told Kalena to go and invite Carmen to our home for a cup of tea. She ran out of the house and down the street with Matthew to his house to invite Carmen up for tea. A few minutes later, here came Kalena, Matthew, and his mom, Carmen. Carmen and I introduced ourselves and sat down and began to talk. The kids took off to Kalena's room to play. Carmen and I just hit it off beautifully. We talked all afternoon.

Several hours had gone by before we knew it. All of a sudden, Rick walked in from work and was surprised to see that I had company. I prayed that he wouldn't say anything stupid because I had a black woman in my home. Carmen rose up and greeted Rick and shook his hand. I introduced them and Matthew. Rick seemed cool with her, and I was glad. Carmen and Matthew left and went home, and Rick surprisingly didn't have a problem with her or Matthew. I really liked Carmen and Matthew. Carmen and I felt like we'd known each other for years after just one afternoon of visiting. We could thank our kids for that one. Carmen and I became fast friends. She was completely accepting of me and my disability. I learned that she also had her own disability. She didn't have any kidney function and went to dialysis three days a week in Kansas City. Plus she had a blood disease called lupus, among some other health issues. As time went on, I also meet Carmen's husband, Matthew, or Big Matt as he was called; the son was Little Matt. I also meet Carmen's mom; her name was Shirley. She worked at the hospital and the local nursing home. She kind of unofficially adopted Kalena and me into her family. Since Kalena's only grandma lived a thousand miles away, Shirley told Kalena that she could call her Grandma. Kalena loved that she had someone close to home that she could call Grandma. Rick and I decided that we needed a second car, and we're doing okay financially. We went to the local car dealership and bought a brand-new car. The loan got approved, and we had chosen a small economical car that got real good gas mileage. Rick informed me that he was going drive the car to work up in the city (Kansas City) because it did get such good gas mileage. I protested because, number one, I wanted to drive it, and, number two, I just knew that he'd get drunk sometime and wreck it. Well, that was exactly what happened five months later. He skipped coming home one night from Kansas City and completely drove past Butler straight south another thirty miles to Nevada, Missouri, to hang out in the bars down there. I got a phone call about one thirty in the morning from the Nevada police, telling me that my husband had been in an accident and had been taken to the Nevada hospital. All I could think about when the officer told me that was, *What about the car?* So I asked the officer about the car. He repeated to me that Rick was in the hospital. I told him that I didn't give a damn about Rick and demanded that he tell me about the car. He proceeded to tell me that the car had rolled five times and was totaled out. Then I asked about Rick. I was told that he was so drunk that all he got was a cut on his head. Well, that just figures; he was too drunk to get hurt very badly, and he was still alive. I really hated this man, and now I had to go and get him. He truly didn't believe that he had a drinking problem. While on the way home from the hospital, I asked him, "Why? What would you have done had you hit someone? What if it had been a family with kids?" His reply was that had he hit someone, they shouldn't have been out there. Then again I asked what if there had been kids involved. What he said next really shocked me. He said that parents shouldn't have their kids out that late at night and that the kids should be home in bed at that hour. Then I said, "What about us? I had to wake up Kalena and bring her with me to come and get your ass." He then told me to shut the hell up and leave him alone. I wished God would put me and Kalena out of our misery and just let him die. We had had four cars, and he had totaled three of them. The insurance that I had to pay for on any car we owned was so high that it was crazy. I was being penalized for his driving. I couldn't keep him from driving. He said that it was his right, and no one was going to tell him that he could not drive. So now that we were down to one car again, I had to hide the keys so he couldn't drive the only car we have left and wrecked it too. His best friend Steve, who lived in Wisconsin and was an over-the-road truck driver, contacted Rick and offered him money to go over the road with him. I told Rick to go with Steve, and he did. I couldn't be happier. Rick said he'd send me some money every couple of weeks. I prayed to God every night that Rick would never come home. I didn't love him, and I didn't want him. While Rick was gone with Steve, Steve's wife, Laurie, called me up out of the blue one night. We got to talking, and she said that since our husbands were together, we might as well get to know each other. Rick had always told me that Laurie was a bitch and that he didn't like her and that I wouldn't like her either.

The person that I was talking to didn't seem to be like that. We began to talk frequently on the phone. I liked her, and she didn't seem to be at all like Rick described her. Rick called me every few days to check in, like I really cared. I didn't tell him that I had been talking with Laurie. After he was gone for two or three months, I finally told him that I didn't want him to ever come home. But here he came anyway. He just didn't get that I didn't love him and didn't want him. He said that I needed him, that I could make it on my own but not with a child. He said, "By yourself maybe but definitely not with a child." He also used the fact that his name was also on the house, so I could not kick him out. We lived more like roommates except when he wanted sex, which was a constant battle in our lives since he's always drunk or drinking. Whenever I did give in, he would ask me if I got off; and when I told him no, then he said that it didn't really matter, because he did and that was all that matters. He said it was my wifely duty to satisfy him sexually. According to him, my wifely duties included keeping the house clean, the laundry, cooking, taking care of the child, and of course sex. I also saw to it that the bills were paid every month, do the shopping, and most generally mow the yard. He would mow occasionally but not very often. His job was to bring home the money, and that was only when he worked, and of course drank his beer. I truly didn't know how people put up with this crap. I didn't know why I did. I did know that this was my house, and I was not leaving it. One night, he came home about dinnertime and drunk as usual. I had just made a pot of spaghetti and sat down with Kalena at the table to eat. He came in stumbling to the table and sat down. Kalena made a remark to him about being drunk, and he grabbed her head and shoved it down into her plate of food and told her to shut her hole. She came up from the plate in shock as I was. She got up started crying and headed to the bathroom to clean up. As she was walking toward the hallway, she yelled, "I hate you, Dad." He jumped up, and I jumped up also. He ran after her saying that he was going to beat her, and I got between the two of them and told him, "I kill you where you stand if you lay one finger on her." I told him to get away from us and just go to bed, and he did. The next morning, he remembered nothing of the night before. He even called me a liar when I told him what had happened. When Kalena told him the same thing that I had, he said that she shouldn't have smarted off to him. Nothing was ever his fault. He blamed everything that he did or said or that was wrong in his life on someone else. He had even told me that the world owed him. When he was at home at night, he sat up all night watching infomercials. He was always sending money to buy those get-rich-quick deals, and they never worked. He had spent hundreds of dollars on all of them. He even got back into the selling of pot again. He said that was where the big money is. He ended up losing more money than he gained. One night, he came home with a bag of weed saying it was some real good stuff and rolled up a joint. After we smoked it, I started feeling strange. I asked him what all was in the weed, and he said nothing but pot. I told him that it had to be laced with something, and he assured me that it was just a superhigh-quality pot that I just hadn't had before.

After a little while, I felt like I was having trouble breathing and began to shake. I asked Rick to help me, and he just said that I was too high. I asked him to take me to the hospital, but he refused, saying I'd have to tell them I had smoked pot and I would end up in jail. I just knew that I was going to die that very night. I was so glad that Kalena was in bed asleep already. Rick kept laughing at me and telling me that I was just too high. I had been smoking pot with him and others for years and had had some extremely high-quality pot in the past that had never made me feel like this. Since I just knew I was probably going to die that night, I went in and sat by Kalena's bed and quietly talked to her while she slept. I then went in my bedroom, crawled into bed, and began to pray to God. I apologized for all my sins and begged his forgiveness. I told God that if he would allow me to wake up tomorrow, I'm going to change my life: I would never smoke pot again and wouldn't allow it in my house anymore, I would change things in my life once and for all, and I would try to be the person I thought I was meant to be, whoever that was supposed to be. Then I turned over to go to sleep not knowing if I would wake up the next morning or not. When the next morning arrived and I woke up, I was so glad and excited for a new life until I realized that I was stark naked. I wasn't that way when I went to bed. I asked Rick why I was naked, and he said that he took my clothes off me and had his way with me. He said it was a real turn on for him. I told him that he had committed rape, and he proceeded to tell me that a wife cannot be raped because she belongs to the husband, and it's her duty to satisfy her husband whenever he wants it. I just couldn't think about that right now. I was alive, and God answered my prayer. From this day forward, there would be no more smoking pot for me, and it wouldn't be allowed in my house. When I told Rick that there would be no more pot in my house, he asked me, "Where's my Bible and badge?" "I am serious," I told him. "If I find pot in this house anywhere, I'll run it down the garbage disposer. I'll flush it down the toilet. It would not remain in my house any longer." I got rid of all the paraphernalia. Rick got really mad, but I didn't care. He could leave, I told him. If he didn't like it, it made no difference to me. When some of our friends came over and wanted to get high with us, Rick said, "She found God and wouldn't allow the stuff in the house any longer." Then the friends asked me, "Where's my Bible? Where's my badge?" I got really sick of it and defending myself. After a while, our so-called friends quit coming around. Go figure. I continued to complain to Rick about his drinking. I talked to God from time to time about Rick. I didn't want to be with him anymore. He wouldn't change or give up the drinking, and I just couldn't take it anymore. I really didn't know what to do. I prayed for help but was not getting any answers. One night, Rick came to me and handed me three envelopes. One was addressed to me, one was addressed to Kalena, and one was to his mom. He told me that I was not to open mine for a few days, and Kalena could have hers when she is older and to mail his mom hers in a few days.

When I asked what was going on, I felt a little excited in the bottom of my stomach; he told me that he was going to kill himself. I told him, "You are not." He said, yes, he was. I told him to go ahead and do it. I told him that nothing would make me happier than to have him gone permanently. He didn't seem surprised by what I said and said that he had it all planned out. He said that he was going downstairs to the garage and attach a piece of garden hose to the muffler pipe of the car the run it into the driver's side window, close the garage door, start the car and sit in the driver's seat, and breath the fumes until he dies. He took me downstairs and showed me what he had rigged up. I thought it's great that by this time tomorrow he would be gone. I knew I shouldn't have felt that way, but I just couldn't feel any other way. I never dreamed that I would be in a marriage like this. He said that I was to just stay upstairs and watch TV like I normally would and then come downstairs tomorrow morning and find him, call the police, and play the part of a grieving wife. He asked me if I would do my part. "Sure, I will," I told him. This latest idea of his really took the cake. He'd take himself out of Kalena's life and mine, and I'd finally be rid of him if he could even go through with it, and I didn't believe for one second that he could or would do it. I thought, *Let's just see how far he would really go with this idea.* I just knew that at some point he was counting on me to put a stop to all that nonsense. He went and spent some time with Kalena before she went to bed. He then tucked her in bed and told her he loved her and came out into the living room and told me how sorry he was for all the things he had done to me and the way he had treated me. He told me that he had always been a screwup all of his life. He said that he knew his parents, especially his mom, were disappointed in him. He told me about all the times he broke into his own parents' home to steal from them because they wouldn't give him any money. He said that he was better off dead to everyone. I just sat there and listened. I couldn't believe that I was actually in my mind agreeing with everything he was saying. He made sure Kalena was asleep; then he told me goodbye and told me that he really did love me and hoped I could find someone else to be with in the future and to make sure that the person is a good father to Kalena. He then gave me a big hug, said goodbye again, and went downstairs. I turned the TV on and started watching it. After a while, I went to check on Kalena, who was sleeping in her room, and as I was heading down the hallway, I realized that because Kalena's room was above the garage, her room smelled of exhaust fumes, and the fumes were also in the hallway. Oh my God, Rick really tried to kill himself, and he was going to take Kalena right along with him. Her room was right above the garage, and some of the fumes had come up into her room—I guess maybe through the furnace vent in there. I had to stop it because the whole back of the house smelled like exhaust fumes. I ran downstairs to the garage and jerked the car door open and told him that I couldn't believe that he was actually doing this and that the fumes were up in Kalena's room, and I turned the car off and took the keys from him. He seemed a little loopy and groggy but fine. I got the garage door open to air it out and ran up to Kalena's room and opened her window to air her room out. I woke her up and told her she needed to go potty, and I got her a drink. I did this just to make sure that she was okay and then put her back to bed. Rick came upstairs and sat on the couch, and I told him that he couldn't even do a good job of killing himself. I asked if he wanted to go to the hospital to get checked out, and he refused. I couldn't help but wonder if he knew all along that I would end up having to come down there because of the fumes in Kalena's room. Was he counting on it? He knew I always went in and checked on Kalena while she slept. So I was wondering if he knew that the fumes would drift up into her room, discover them when I'd go to look in on her, and race down to put a stop to all this? I asked him, and he just looked at me. "How sick of a man are you?" I asked. Again, he had no response. "I cannot believe I married a sick and twisted man like you," I told him. I finally went to bed, and he slept on the couch.

The next morning, he acted like nothing had ever happened. What happened the night before was never brought up or discussed ever again. We had only one full-service gas station in town. All the others in town were self-service stations with little stores inside. I always went to the full-service station to get gas so that I didn't have to pump the gas myself. I didn't even have to get out of the car to do anything. They would do it all for you. They would wash your windows and check your tires and your oil if you asked them to. The man who owned the station, Mr. C, and his male employee, George, were very nice men. Every time I pulled into the station, George came out with a big smile on his face and was so friendly. He couldn't seem to do enough for me—always wanted to know if there was anything else he could do for me. Over time, as we got to know one another, I came to the realization that George was interested in me and me in him. He was a married man with kids, and I was a married woman, although unhappily, with a child of my own. I found myself searching for reasons to stop at the station just to visit with him. He was so fascinating to me. I really enjoyed talking with him. He told me the same thing. Then, one day, he said he wanted to get together alone with me and asked me if I would like to be alone with him. I told him yes but asked where and how, since we're both married and it was a small town. He then asked me if I could get away some evening and meet him outside of town. "I'll meet you. Just tell me where and when," I told him. We set a date to meet at 9:00 p.m. on a road outside of town. I called my friend Carmen and asked her to cover for me, and she agreed, and I told Rick that Carmen wasn't feeling well and that I was going to go and sit with her for a while. They had since moved from down the street to across town, so I had to take the car, which left him at home with Kalena and with no car. Rick knew that Carmen had been having health issues, so he didn't even question it. Besides, he didn't even suspect that any man other than himself would be interested in me, so everything was a go. I did go to Carmen's house before I went to meet George. Carmen knew about all the trouble I'd had with Rick and understood and supported me. I met George outside of town, and we went in his car several more miles out into the country. It's the middle of summer. It's very hot out, and George pulled up to this small pond on someone's property. The moon and stars were out and brightly shinning on the water. This was so pretty and romantic.

George pulled out a blanket and spread it on the ground. We lay down on it under the moon and stars. My heart was just racing; it felt like it was going to beat out of my chest. I hadn't felt this in years. This was coming from someone who hated sex, and at that moment, all I wanted was to have George make love to me right here and right now.

I knew then that it's not me who had a problem sexually; I just was not sexually attracted to Rick. We lay there talking, and then all of a sudden, George leaned over and kissed me. His kisses were gentle and tender. After a while, he began to undress me, and I undressed him, and the passion exploded between us. Afterward, I lay there in his arms completely content. When it's finally time to head back to town, neither one of us wanted to go. George said that he definitely wanted to see me again if I wanted it too. I did want to see him again,

I told him. When I got back to town, I went straight to Carmen and visited and told her about everything. She's happy for me and told me to just be very careful and reminded me that it was a very small town.

When I finally got home, Rick asked me how Carmen was, and I told him that she was resting comfortably when I left her. He jokingly said, "I'll bet you weren't really with her, were you?" I thought for a second and then said, "You're right. I was actually in the country by a pond on a blanket, making mad passionate love to another man under the moon and stars." He looked at me and then started laughing and said, "In your dreams. You hate sex, and, besides, no man would ever want to f——k a crippled bitch like you, and if he does, then it's just to find out what it's like to f——k someone like you." I'd heard this statement so many times from him. But whenever I said, "What about you?" He said, "But I love you." I told him, "With love like that, I certainly don't need enemies." I've got to find a way to get him out of my life. It's funny, though; I did actually tell him the truth about where I was, and even what I was doing, and he didn't even believe me. The next time I saw George, he asked me if Rick said anything to me about that night. I told him that I had told Rick the truth about that night. For a moment, George turned white as a sheet, and his eyes were as big as plates when I explained everything, and he couldn't believe it. He was really shocked to learn that Rick was told the truth—the whole truth, and he didn't even believe it. Well, at least, I could say in all honesty that I did not lie to Rick about what I was doing that night. But then I wondered why George really wanted to be with me. I wondered if it like Rick said, that men were just curious about someone like me. Well, if that were the case, then he wouldn't have said he wanted to see me again, would he? I didn't know what to think. I wondered if men were really like what Rick had been telling me all those years. I was not much good at judging a man. That much was very obvious by the man I married. If I'd known all this about Rick prior to marriage, I would never have married him. Well, I just couldn't think about that right now. As the days and weeks passed, all I could think about was George and how much I wanted to see him again. I was always driving by the station when he worked, just hoping to get a glimpse of him. I knew that I couldn't stop there constantly, or his boss may become suspicious, so I drove by frequently when I was out and about. Whenever we did see each other, he did wave at me, and I also got a wink from him that made my heart just leap with joy. I didn't know when we'd get to be alone again, but the occasional wave and wink I got from him satisfied me.

What little spending money I did have, and it certainly wasn't much, I tried to take Kalena and do something with her. Rick never wanted to go with us to do anything, so she and I went alone. There was a drive-in movie there in town, and kids twelve and under got in free, and an adult ticket was three dollars. I took stuff from the house to drink and our own popcorn and went to watch movies at the drive-in. Kalena and I really enjoyed this time together. Sometimes, George brought his two youngest kids to the movies, and we parked beside each other in the back row. My daughter and his daughter were the same age, so they sometimes liked to sit together. I always arrived a little early so that Kalena could go and play on the playground equipment they had there until the movie started. Sometimes, George came a little early too, and his kids went and played also. Whenever that did happen, we stayed in our own cars but could talk to each other through the windows. No one could accuse us of anything because we're just friends visiting from our cars. He told me that the one time we were together just wasn't enough for him and if the time was right we'd be together again. I was cool with that because I was a patient person. I enjoyed just getting to know him. Meanwhile, back on the home front, Rick said that I'd never be able to get rid of him. I'd made up my mind that that was exactly what I was going to do.

Now just to figure out how to make him leave. After considerable thought, I decided that I was going to live my life from here on out as if he wasn't here. I decided that he did not exist, not to me and not in my home. So then began my new life without him. I thought, *Every day, from now on, I'll live as if he isn't here. I'll totally ignore him. Why? Because he doesn't exist. He is not here.* That was how I decided I would live my life. When I got up in the morning, I make just enough coffee for me. When I cooked, I only made enough food for me and Kalena. I refused to answer him when he spoke to me, because he wasn't here to me. I bought only enough food to feed two people, Kalena and me. I took Kalena almost daily somewhere, so we didn't have to be in the house around him. One day, he got so mad at Kalena because she was crying because he yelled that she was an air-headed bitch just like me and would grow up to be just as worthless as me. By then, I'd been ignoring Rick for about a month, but when he started in on an impressionable young child with the crap that I'd taken from him for years, something inside of me snapped. He could say whatever he wanted to me; I had broad shoulders, and I could take it. But when he started in on my child, this impressionable little girl, then that was where I had to drew the line. I just snapped, and the mama lion, the mama grizzly bear, the she coon—whatever it was—came out in me; and I ordered him out of the house and out of my life with such rage that he knew he had no other choice but to leave. I could only imagine the look that was on my face that he saw. I'd never felt such rage before except the time when he was drunk and went after her because she said she hated him. He said that he'd go but that he would be back. He told me that I couldn't make it on my own, not with a child. He said that if I were by myself, then I would be okay, but since I had a child, I wouldn't be able to make it without his help. "I've been making it on just my Social Security half of our marriage because you don't always work, so how dare you tell me that I couldn't make it by myself?" I told him. He said it would only take a few months, but then I would be begging him to come back and that he'd be back. That's when I told him, "I'll do whatever it takes even if I have to sell my soul to make it without you. I promise you that I would never call you or beg you for anything in life, and that's a promise you could bank on. Now pack your shit and get out." I never felt as empowered as I did at that moment. I didn't know that I had that in me. I guess it's true what they say about a mama lion, or mama bear. I rose up to protect my young. I had an inner strength that I didn't know was there. As time passed, I found that I was completely comfortable without Rick. Kalena and I were doing just fine.

She didn't even ask about her dad or where he was. I guess it was because he wasn't even there most of the time, anyway, and she got used to it. One day, I got a letter in the mail stating that my house would up for sale soon on the courthouse steps for back taxes. Oh my gosh, that SOB left me with unpaid property taxes on the house. I called the courthouse and discovered that he never paid the taxes at all and my house would be sold if I couldn't come up with nearly $1,000 within a few weeks. I was at a total loss; I didn't have that kind of money and didn't know where I would get it. I just knew that Rick somehow knew this would happen and was expecting me to call him for help. "Well, I will not do it," I told myself. I didn't know what I was going to do, but I thought something would come up. One night, while watching TV, I saw a commercial for Rolox windows. A lightbulb went off in my head. I had an idea that might just work, and if it didn't, then I was no worse off than I was right now. I call the 800 number and asked for a representative to call on me. Within a day or two, a man from Rolox showed up at my house with his demos in tow. He went through his demonstration, and when he was done, I told him that I would purchase some of the Rolox windows under two conditions. He then asked what the two conditions are, and I told him that I want triple-pane windows at a double-pane price, and I wanted Rolox to pay my back taxes and add the back taxes amount to my bill. I would then make payments to Rolox until everything is paid in full however long it takes. He told me that he's pretty sure Rolox would not go for something like that. I told him that those were my conditions, take it or leave it. He called the company and told them about my conditions; and after a lengthy conversation with the company, and to my surprise and shock, Rolox agreed to my conditions; and of course I got everything in writing. Within a few days, I received confirmation that my taxes were paid, and a few weeks later, Rolox arrived to install my triple-pane windows at double-pane price. I just knew that Rick probably never expected me to be able to hold onto this house. I was a good housekeeper. I got rid of the husband and kept the house. I got word to George that I was officially alone now and was available whenever he could get away. My grandma and granddad Rye always told me if you don't have your word, then you have nothing. People didn't really know me in this little town, but I've got to find a way to build a good reputation based on my word here. As time went by, I found that there were things I needed from time to time, but I didn't always have the money at the time of need. So I went to the hardware store or the plumbing store or wherever I needed to go for a part or whatever the need was; explained to them that I was buying a government house, that I lived on a fixed income but needed whatever it was; and asked if I could come in on the third of the upcoming month and pay for those things I needed. One by one, the stores ended up taking me at my word and trusting me. I thought I would keep my word to them no matter what. On the third, I always paid them back their money so that in the future if I needed to use them again they would trust me. Nothing felt better to me than to know that I was a woman of my word. When I give you my word, then you could bank on it. I'd even had to get tires for my car based on my word. I never let anyone down. Always paid when I said I would. People learned that I could be counted on and trusted. I started ordering all the *Time-Life* how-to books off TV. I needed to learn how to do things around my house because I couldn't pay someone to come here and do the work for me whatever it was.

Besides I am not a stupid woman. I knew that I could do whatever I needed to. I changed my own oil and oil filter in my car. I could even do a general tune-up. I got Kalena to help me with things so she could learn as well, and to see her mama do things for herself without any man's help. I wanted her to grow up self-sufficient and dependent upon herself. The one thing that I just truly didn't really mess with was electricity; I wondered why, ha, ha! Those how-to books were so easy to follow, and the step-by-step pictures were great too. They were some of the best books around for a homeowner and person like me who wanted to do minor things on my own. During one of my conversations with George, I found out that he went bowling every week, and even worked at the local bowling alley occasionally. He asked me if I bowled, and I told him no. I actually hadn't bowled in years and was never any good at it, anyway. He told me that I should try it and suggested that I get on the mixed league.

So I went out to the bowling alley and found out about it and the cost. I signed up for the Friday night mixed league. I explained to them that I only get paid once a month and that I would pay for the whole month at once, instead of weekly like everyone else. No one had a problem with that. I discovered that I really liked bowling and the being around other people, and conversing was great. I was having so much fun bowling and improving weekly. Different people helped me with my stance and swinging of my arm. Kalena always went with me and played with the other kids there. It's our weekly routine that we both enjoyed. I also learned how to keep the bowling score. Our bowling alley was not automated, and each score must be written down on the score sheets and added up as the games went on. It took me a while to learn it, but I finally mastered it. I was then approached about signing Kalena up for the youth bowling league on Saturdays. After discussing it with Kalena, I signed her up and then volunteered to keep score for the kids on Saturday. Most parents just dropped their kids off on Saturday morning and left. There weren't enough adults to keep score for the kids, so sometimes I was running from lane to lane to write the scores down. Some of the older kids could write the score down but didn't know how to add them up, so I added up them later as long as they could write them down. I did get angry that parents won't get involved in their kids' lives more. They'll pay for their child to be in sports and then just drop them off and leave. I just didn't get how they could do that. Kalena also played T-ball and soccer. My thinking was that if I kept her so involved in activities and sports, then she wouldn't have time to get into drugs. I watched a lot of talk shows on TV, one of which was the *Sally Jessy Raphael Show*. She always had single moms on there who were afraid of their children or whose child was out of control or whose child abused them. I thought to myself, *Over my cold dead body would I ever fear my child.* I was the adult and the boss. I would not have an out-of-control, disrespectful, disobedient, or rude child. She would have manners, values, and morals, and would be polite. She would use the words "Please," "Thank you," "Yes, ma'am," "No, ma'am," "Yes, sir," and "No, sir." The day I'd fear my child, well, it's just not going to happen. I didn't care if I had to get on a chair and use a bat.

I would not fear my child or any other child for that matter. Kalena learned early on that I was a woman of my word. She learned that if I promised a punishment, she got it. I also learned to be very careful what I promised to her or anyone else, because good or bad, I'd have to carry through with it because I gave my word. My dad used to whistle real loud to call us kids home. Kalena played over at the park a lot or around the neighborhood. I couldn't yell loud enough for her to hear me, so I told her that I would whistle real loud and, when she hears the whistle, to come home. Boy, I could whistle very loud. I was the only one in the area who whistled like that, and everyone in the neighborhood knew my whistle. Within a few minutes, Kalena came running to check in. Sometimes, when I whistled, I'd hear someone yell, "Kalena, your mom is calling you." I really got a kick out of that. It really made me laugh. My daughter was a trip, though. We lived right across the street from the park, and one day, she actually asked me to please drive her to the park. I asked her if she had lost her mind. She said no, that she just didn't want to walk. Oh, well, I told her, "If you want to go, then walk." She said that she wanted to go to the other side, and it was too far to walk across. Talk about lazy, she only asked the one time and then never again. I just couldn't believe she actually wanted me to drive her around the block to the other side of the park. There were so many kids in the neighborhood that Kalena played with, and most of them were boys. She was just one of the boys as far as they were concerned. She played football, soccer, climbed trees, helped build forts, rode bikes, and even occasionally got into fights with these boys. I really didn't think some of them realized that she was a girl. She had short hair and always wore a ball cap, blue jeans, and tee shirts. One day, she came to me and told me there was a family on the street behind us that was real nice and wanted me to meet them. She said they had two boys and that she played with the older one in the neighborhood.

One day, while I was out working on the brakes of my car, I was in need of a C-clamp but didn't have one. Kalena told me that the man behind us probably had one that I could borrow. I sent her over to ask, and he told her that, yes, he had one and that I could borrow it. He asked her if I needed any help, and she told him no. When I got finished changing my brake pads, I returned the C-clamp to the neighbor and meet him and his family. David and Stacey and their boys, Kevin and Scott, seemed like a very nice family. Kalena was a couple of years older than Kevin, but they played well together. Since I no longer smoked pot, I had taken up drinking a little whiskey. I just drank it straight out of the bottle and chased it with my tea, since I was a tea drinker. I usually bought a half-pint bottle and drank on Saturday nights alone. Kalena was usually spending the night with someone on Saturdays, so she's not there to see me drink alcohol. I felt she had enough of that with her dad. I really missed the "high" feeling I got from smoking pot, so I found myself drinking to get that "high" feeling again. The only thing is that with drinking, you have a hangover feeling the next day that pot doesn't give you.

As time went by, I found myself drinking more and more but never around Kalena. Sometimes, I drank in the morning after Kalena had gone to school and after I had had my morning coffee. I just really needed that buzz to get me going. When I used to smoke pot, I would periodically smoke it throughout the day to get buzzed. At that point, I was drinking to do the same thing since I quit smoking pot. I was a good mom, though. My house was clean, laundry was done, meals were cooked, and yard was mowed. Everything was done to and around my home and for my child. One day, George asked me if I'd like to go to Springfield for a day. "Heck, yes," I told him. I'd never been there before. I got Kalena lined up with friends for the day, and I was so nervous that I went and bought a bottle of whiskey to help me with my nerves. On the way there, I asked George if he would mind if I drank it, and he said, no, not at all. I offered some to him, but he refused. He took me to a place called Bass Pro Shop. The place was huge, and I'd never been there either. Oh my goodness, this place was so neat. We spent quite a while there and even had lunch there. Later, George rented a nice motel room where we spent the afternoon. I really didn't want the day to end, but it did, and we went back home. He said that we'd get together again soon. I couldn't wait. Later, George told me that his wife would be going to college three days a week and that he would come by on his lunch breaks from work. She attended school on Mondays,

Wednesday, and Fridays. Usually, at least two of the three days, he came over to my house. Some days, I fixed him lunch, and other days, we had crazy sex for lunch. He did things to me that I'd never done before. He made me feel so good. He asked me questions that no one had ever asked me before. Except him, no one ever asked me what my goals were or my desires.

George even asked me what my fantasies were. I'd never thought about that before. I didn't have any fantasies, or at least I'd never given that any thought. I guess I didn't know that I could have any. I guess I thought those were for other people and not for me. As the months went by, George also took me to play bingo up toward Kansas City. I'd never seen bingo played this way before. They tried to build pictures playing bingo. It's confusing to me, but I just enjoyed being with him for a few hours. I really enjoyed our times together, but they were not enough sometimes. I would like to have more but knew that that wasn't going to happen. I had come to realize that I was in love with George and couldn't have him. I wanted to let him go but couldn't. I knew I should end things with him, but I just couldn't. I knew that one of these days we'd probably get caught. Then I thought maybe if that happened and she left him, then he'd be free to be with me. My mind was all over the place where he was concerned. Then, one day. I learned that I was pregnant with his baby. I didn't know what to do. I was not supposed to be able to get pregnant. I just didn't know what to do now. *Do I tell him or not? He'll know eventually, and he knows that there isn't anyone else I was seeing.* A part of me was thrilled that I was having another baby, but also I didn't want another one, on the other hand.

How do I tell him this news? What would his thoughts and feelings be on this? After a few weeks, I finally got up enough nerve to go to the station and tell him, but before I could tell him, he guessed it. He said he'd try to do what he could, but he could never admit the baby was his to anyone. My heart sank to the ground, and I was devastated. A few days later, his wife showed up at my house in the middle of the night, banging on my door. She told me to stay away from her husband, and if I didn't, then I could be in a car wreck or something bad could happen to me. She said that accidents happen every day to people, and I could find myself in one. About that time, Kalena came walking down the hall, wanting to know what all the shouting was all about. His wife apologized for waking up Kalena and warned me again; then she left. In the meantime, I got a call from my brother David. He was getting married and wanted me and Kalena to attend his wedding in Wichita. He said that he would put me and Kalena up at his place while we were there. I asked him about Dad and if he intended to invite him, and he said yes. I hadn't seen my father since Kalena was eleven months old, and she was eight years old then. She didn't even know who my dad was or Betty either. At David's wedding, Dad and Betty did show up. After the wedding, I tried to make a quick exit so as not to have a confrontation with them. I was stopped outside by other guests, and Dad and Betty came up to me and said hello. I introduced Kalena to them, but she stayed behind me, not wanting to speak. David and Tammy and I were all standing outside the chapel, talking with Dad and Betty when out of the blue Betty invited us out to their place for a visit. Instantly, David and I turned around and looked behind us to see whom she was talking to and realized that she was talking to us. We looked at each other in shock and accepted the invitation. After the reception, we all went out there and visited with them. We just couldn't believe Betty invited us out there and wondered where that came from. We were glad, though, and I gave them my phone number and address, and David gave them his. What a surprise this was to David and me. I decided not to tell Dad and Betty about my pregnancy; I didn't want any of the questions they would have. If Betty found out about my situation, she would be very judgmental and probably cut me out of Dad's life again. I didn't need or want that. I was not even sure if I was back in Dad's life permanently or not. After I reached my fifth month of pregnancy, I went into premature labor. Kalena ended up staying with Carmen and Matthew, while I ended up in the hospital in Kansas City. The doctors stopped my labor but kept me in the hospital. Kalena had never seen me in a hospital. A week later, Carmen brought Kalena to the hospital for a visit, and when Kalena saw me hooked up to all the machines and all the tubes, she completely freaked out and ran out of the room. Carmen explained everything to Kalena and brought her back in the room for me to see her. I never wanted to see that look on my daughter's face again. Nine days into my hospital stay, I went into labor again. This time, the doctors couldn't stop it. I ended up delivering a baby girl. Kaitlyn Leeann was born February 19.

She weighed one pound and was twelve inches long and lived about an hour and a half.

Doctors tried everything they could to keep her alive, but her heart and lungs weren't strong enough to sustain life. I was numb. I knew that she was a blessing, on one hand; but, on the other hand, I'd just lost my baby—a baby whom I wasn't sure I wanted because of the circumstances I was in but would have loved anyway.

Nurses came and asked me what I wanted done with the body. I couldn't afford a funeral, I told them. They told me that I could sign some papers, and they would cremate the body for me. So that's what I did. They brought her to me to spend time with her before the cremation. She was absolutely perfectly whole. She had all ten fingers and all ten toes. She even had fingernails and toenails. She was so beautiful and so very tiny. Her head was about the size of a tennis ball, and her arms and legs were about the size of my finger. I just held her for the longest time and sobbed my heart out. *How am I leaving here empty-handed? How do I go on without her?* I was so alone and had no one to share this grief with. George didn't even know I went to the hospital, much less that his child died. *Do I even tell him when I get home? Would he even care?*

My head knew that it was a blessing, but my heart didn't think so. Carmen reminded me that I still had a child who needed her mama. Carmen was right, and once again, it's just Kalena and me against the world. After twelve days in the hospital, I was released to go home. Carmen came and took me home. I felt so empty. I went to the hospital and had a baby, but I came home empty-handed. I got home on a Saturday, and when Kalena asked about the baby, her baby sister, I told her that her baby sister went to heaven. She took it very hard, harder than I thought she would. She's mad at me now because she didn't get to see Kaitlyn or to say goodbye to her sister. I had never felt more alone in my life. I had no family to help me through this; I didn't even have George for support. Kalena needed me, but I also needed to grieve my loss. I thought, *How do I stay strong for Kalena and grieve too?*

Monday morning rolled around, and I got Kalena up and off to school. While sitting and staring out the window, I saw the world going on outside. I realized that the world was not going to stop because of my grief. I was in pain, and the world kept on going. I started drinking again to numb my pain. I had quit while I was pregnant, but that time seemed like a good time to start again. I was drinking every day then and getting pretty buzzed all the time. The neighbor up the street had three girls, and he took his girls and Kalena to school every morning and it's my job to pick everyone up from school and bring them home in the afternoon. I always made sure I was sober by the afternoon to get the girls. One day, while watching TV, I saw a commercial about a mom who was drunk and passed out on the couch while her daughter was calling home from school wondering where she was. The little girl was crying into the phone, saying, "Mom, where are you? Why don't you answer the phone?" It was like someone had just slapped me in the face. I was becoming that mom. I had never seen that commercial before, but it sure sobered me up fast, and I quit drinking.

Kalena kept telling me that she missed her sister and wished she could talk to her. I wished I could talk to Katy as we called her too. I told Kalena to write a letter to Katy and say everything in the letter that she would say in person if she could, and I did the same thing. After we wrote our letters to Katy, I got out our BBQ grill and lit it up. After the coals got good and hot, I put the letters in the fire and told Kalena that the ashes would take the words up to heaven to Katy and that God would read them to her. That really seemed to help Kalena a lot, and it helped me too. One day, Kalena told me that when she grows up, she wants to be like me and stay home and take care of her house and collect Social Security just like I did. I was proud that she wanted to be like me but was shocked that she wanted to collect Social Security. All I could think of was, *What kind of example am I setting for her?* I hated that that was how she saw me. I thought, *This has to change. I have got to find some kind of a part-*

time job. One day, I was in our local Hardees getting a sandwich when I saw a neighbor of mine, Eric, working in the kitchen there. While waiting on my food, I stood and chatted with Eric. Later that afternoon, Eric stopped by my house with an application and said that the manager Mary had watched me talking to him earlier and was impressed with me and would like to hire me if I wanted a job. I couldn't believe the timing of that offer. I filled out the application and took it back to Mary at the restaurant a couple of days later. She interviewed me, and one of the questions she asked me was what my greatest accomplishment besides my child? The answer was an easy one for me, the day I changed the brake pads on my car all by myself. That was my greatest accomplishment to date, besides my child. I had always been proud of the fact that I did things for myself in spite of my disability. I wanted my daughter to see that I could do anything if I put my mind to it, and I wanted her to be proud of me and never ashamed of me. I didn't need anything from anyone, and I could do all things on my own. Mary hired me that very day. I had never worked in the food industry in my life. I explained to her that according to the paperwork from Social Security, I was limited as to how much money I could make.

Mary was willing to work with me on that issue. She also understood that I was a single mom and I couldn't and would not work at night. It took about two weeks for me to get the hang of this job, and the restaurant just happened to be right across the street from the gas station where George worked. My daughter had become a latchkey child. I had given her very strict instructions as to what she could and couldn't do at home while alone. I even tested her at times to make sure she was obeying my rules. I usually worked from 11:00 a.m. to 5:00 p.m., so she was home about an hour and a half alone before I got there. I told her the door must be kept locked at all times until I got home, she absolutely couldn't answer the phone or door, and no friends were to be allowed in the house while I was gone. There should absolutely be no cooking, and the stove must not be turned on. Homework was to be done before I got home. Mary asked me if I would be willing to do some opening shifts, 6:00 a.m. to 1:00 p.m. I told Mary that I could, but I knew I would have to get Kalena up earlier and bring her to work with me on those days. The grade school was right behind Hardees Restaurant, and Kalena didn't have far to walk. So on the days that I had to open the restaurant, Kalena came with me. She got a nice hot breakfast and watched me work until she had to go to school. I thought this was good for her to see her mama in action at work and how I dealt with and handled my customers. I discovered that I loved working at this job. I loved dealing with the public, and I was good at it. I'd discovered that I was a people person, and they responded very well to me. This was also the first time I'd ever worked with money and a cash register. With this job, I was gaining a confidence I'd never had, and I felt like I was coming into my own person, whoever that was supposed to be. I grew to love my customers, most of them anyway, and they seemed to have really taken to me. Even with my one arm, I often carried the tray of food and drink for the very elderly—the ones with walkers or who shake a little too much to try and carry something. They were truly grateful to me for doing it, but it was my pleasure also. I truly didn't mind helping them or anyone else in need. I would hope one day it would be done for me if needed. I always thought that most people working in fast food were teenagers or people who couldn't really work anywhere else, or even bimbos. While working at Hardees, I quickly learned that I was very wrong. One really needs to be a people person to do that job. You must also be quick thinking and quick on your feet, as well as friendly at all times. A bimbo could not do that job. I also learned that a person could absolutely support a family working fast food. You may not get rich, but as long as you don't live above your means, you could live a decent life. Case in point was my good friends: Eric, who brought me the application; his wife, Becky; and their two sons, Corey and Cody.

They were an extremely beautiful family and good friends for anyone to have. They also just happened to be some of my neighbors, and good ones at that. As time went on, I became friendlier with David and Stacey and their boys. I also met a woman who lived on the street behind me named Lora, whom I didn't care too much for. She also had two kids, a boy and girl, and she also hung out at and with David and Stacey. I refused to be around her, and whenever she was at David and Stacey's, I wouldn't go over there, even if invited. In my opinion, she was loud and obnoxious, and a lousy mom too. Her kids ran wildly all over the neighborhood, and the little girl was only three. One day, I heard a child screaming outside my house, so I went out to see what was going on. I found that little girl sitting in the middle of the street butt-ass naked and screaming to the top of her lungs. When I approached her to see what was wrong, she got up and ran off down the street. I looked up and down the street for an adult, any adult, and saw no one in sight anywhere. What mother lets her three-year-old child run like that? I truly just didn't like her or her mothering skills or lack thereof. I'd a good mind to go and beat that woman's ass myself. I just couldn't believe her. Did she not realize how easy it would be for her child to get kidnapped? Well, I soon discovered that David and Stacey were big football fans.

They watched the Kansas City Chiefs football games on Sundays. They even had football watching parties. I got invited to one of their game-watching parties. I didn't know anything about football at all, but I went to socialize. This became an every Sunday ritual. Sometimes, I even hosted it at my house. David was real good at explaining the game, and they played to me so that I could learn the game. I was actually learning the game and enjoying it too. I got right in there and yelled at the players and the refs, and cheered and booed with everyone. I kinda liked this game. It's something that I never grew up with, and Rick was never into football or any other sports. As time went by, David and Stacey became my best friends, and even invited me and Kalena to their family gatherings, and even their family holidays. David's mom even said that I was her unofficially adopted daughter. I just loved David's mom; she was a real neat lady. I guess she didn't warm up to a lot of people, but she had certainly warmed up to me. After a while, David began introducing me as his sister to people we met, and I began doing the same. Eventually, people in the town knew David and me as brother and sister. It's kinda funny, though, that I told people I had two brothers both named David, and one just happened to be unofficially adopted. I eventually told David and Stacey about George, and they even watched Kalena for me sometimes when George and I were going to get together. I was still involved in bowling, and even got Stacey on the bowling league. That became our weekly ritual. Over time, George and I eventually drifted apart, and I met Greg. He was single and very cute. He noticed me first and just couldn't seemed stay away from me.

He was constantly coming to my house to visit. After a while, we began to date, and I really enjoyed his company. We didn't have to hide either; we could be in public for all to see. Kalena said she really liked Greg, and he seemed to get along with her. Greg has two kids of his own, a boy and girl, so he was able to get along with Kalena easily. I didn't know how it happened, but the gal Lora, who lived on the street behind me whom I couldn't stand, she and I had become friends. Actually, Stacey and Lora were friends, and Stacey made Lora and me sit down and discuss our issues, and we came away as friends. Never saw that one coming, but Lora and I actually became quite close, surprise, surprise. Lora called me every morning just to say good morning. Wow, who'd a thunk it? We all—David, Stacey, Greg, Lora, and I—started hanging out together, almost daily. We played a lot of cards, mostly Skipbo. Everyone I was around now seemed to smoke pot. It was offered to me, but I declined it. Then I was asked if I'd ever tried it. I told them yes and that I smoked it for years, and I told them what happened the last time I smoked it. I told them that I felt that it was laced with something and that I thought I was going to die, so I quit. They continued offering it to me over time, telling me that they would never lace it and that I would be perfectly safe. After weeks of declining it, I finally give in but become paranoid that something bad would happen, but that eventually passed. I finally just went home and took a nap to sleep it off. I must admit that after I awoke, I realized that I had missed getting high. I liked that high feeling one gets from pot. It's like getting buzzed from alcohol, but it's different. I liked it, and I wanted to smoke some more. I knew I shouldn't, but I did. I knew it's been five years since I made that promise to God, but I broke it anyway. As time went on, I became a "pothead" again. I still worked, took care of my household, paid my bills on time, and took care of my daughter. In fact, I ended up helping Lora with her kids frequently.

She seemed to get stressed out a lot with them, and I went over to her house to give her a break from them and maybe even them a break from her until she could get herself calmed down. Sometimes, I sent her into the bathroom to take a long hot relaxing bath, and I tended to the kids. She and I sat up sometimes to the wee hours of the morning playing cards on days that we didn't work. David and Stacey went on canoe trips every summer with his sister Denise and brother-in-law Brian. I'd never even heard of canoe trips. They told me that it's a quite fun and relaxing camping/canoe trip weekend. Over time, I finally met one of David's sisters, that one being Denise and her husband, Brian, and their two beautiful kids, Kelly and Michael. They lived in Kansas City and came down to Butler from time to time and visited with David, Stacey, their boys, and David's mom, who was also Denise's mom too. One day, Kelly, their daughter who was about three or four years old at the time, couldn't remember my name, and she was trying very hard to get my attention, but I didn't realize it. I was walking across the street to head to my house when, all of a sudden, I heard a voice yell out, "Hey, Broken-arm Lady!" That stopped me dead in my tracks, and I turned around to see who said that, and it was Kelly. Denise and Brian were in shock to hear their daughter say that and jumped up to scold her immediately. I, in turn, immediately stopped them from doing so. I explained that what Kelly said was perfectly fine with me—that she was only trying to get my attention the only way she knew how and I was not at all offended. In fact, I was extremely impressed with her for coming up with that. I could, however, understand their embarrassment, but reassured them that I was okay with it. We became good friends also. When the holidays rolled around, David invited me and Kalena to have Thanksgiving dinner at his sister Denise's house. So we attended and were just accepted right into their family as well. I really like Denise and Brian and their kids. The kids ended up calling me Aunt Diana, which was cool with me. The next summer, I got invited to go with everyone on the canoe/camping trip. The weekend trip was strictly an all-adults weekend only, no kids allowed. They told me that they'd pair me with someone who could paddle the canoe for me. A few days before the trip, Kalena fell off a neighbor's back porch. Some of the kids came and told me that Kalena was hurt. So I went to check things out. When I got to where she was at, I found her lying on the ground crying and noticed right away that her arm was in kind of an *S* shape. I realized that her arm was broken. After I assessed the situation and made sure nothing else was hurt or broken, I took her to the emergency room to get her arm casted. They told me that she would have to be put out in order for them to straighten out the bone before they could put a cast on it. So she was in the hospital overnight. I told David and Stacey that I couldn't go on the trip because of Kalena's injury, but they insisted that I could go, and David's mom volunteered to keep Kalena and their boys that weekend, so all was a go now. The campgrounds we went to was way down in southern Missouri. The place was really beautiful and peaceful. We got all our tents and equipment set up at our campsite and gathered up wood for our campfire. I hadn't been camping since Debbie and I went years ago. I really loved being out in nature like this. The actual canoe trip was in the morning; so tonight we sat around and ate, visited, talked, and just relaxed. The person they had me paired with in a canoe was the brother of a friend of theirs. Their friend had told her brother that he had better not let anything happen to me, or he would answer to her. She then told me that I was in very capable hands and to just sit back and enjoy the ride down the river.

We all got around the next morning bright and early. We got breakfast over with and got all the coolers loaded up for the day with lunch stuff, drinks, and munchies, etc… and headed for the river. After everyone got into their canoes, we're off and paddling. This was so cool; I'd never done anything like this. I was so excited that I could almost burst. As we're going along, I began to notice that the guy paddling our canoe was keeping us a little ways away from everyone else.

Everyone was splashing each other and shooting different ones with super soakers. Everyone except us was getting wet and having fun. When he told his sister he wouldn't let anything happen to me and that he would take care of me, he meant it literally. He wouldn't even let us get close enough to anyone else to get splashed. So I said something to him about that. I told him that although I had one arm and an artificial leg, I was not made of sugar, and I would not melt. I continued to tell him that I wanted to be up with the group, so please stop being so overly protective of me. I also told him that as long as he paddled the canoe and didn't let us tip over, I'd be just fine. So after a while, he relaxed enough to actually enjoy the trip. Occasionally, I did splash him with some water. Partway down the river, some people started throwing something called Jell-O shots at us. I'd never heard of these before. They were little plastic containers with a shot of Jell-O inside that was made with alcohol. Oh my goodness, these were so delicious. Stacey and I found out from the others how they were made so our next trip would include them. The scenery going down the river was just beautiful. The entire trip was about six to eight hours. Along the way, we stopped and played in the water, had a type of picnic lunch, and just had a wonderful time. I already knew that this couldn't be my last trip. I thought, *I must do this again in the future.* Later that day, when we finally arrived back at camp, everyone was exhausted. Some of us went and took naps, some gathered wood for the nighttime campfire, and some went and showered and cleaned up. The rest of the evening was spent sitting around the campfire, eating and drinking alcohol. Some of us were getting high, some were not. We all talked and told stories until the wee hours of the morning. When morning arrived, everyone was moving a little slowly. Most of us were pretty sunburned, some were hung over, but mostly we were just very tired. It's been a fun and exciting weekend, but a very exhausting one. We had to get breakfast and then get the camp taken apart and everything packed and loaded up for the long drive home. I did wonder occasionally over the weekend how Kalena was doing, but I knew that with David's mom she would be fine. This weekend's canoe float trip was awesome, and I couldn't wait to go on another one someday.

Later that year, Kalena got sick. I didn't think too much about it, thinking that it's probably the flu. She was running a temperature and throwing up. She then began to have diarrhea and was getting worse by the day. She's in the bathroom sitting on the toilet with diarrhea and throwing up in the trash can. After four days and with no signs of getting any better—in fact she was worse—I took her to the emergency room, where she was promptly admitted to the hospital. Her temp kept going up. The hospital was scrambling to bring the fever down. Every time they gave her something by mouth, she threw it up. They then gave her some kind of a suppository to bring her fever down, but with the diarrhea, that didn't work either. I knew from all my years of experiences with hospitals that nurses couldn't tell you any information about what was wrong. Only a doctor could give you information. Whenever I asked the doctor what he thought was wrong with Kalena, he treated me and talked to me like I was an idiot. He blew me off, and even told me I wouldn't understand. I began asking the nurses what was wrong with my daughter, knowing they couldn't tell me, but needing answers anyway. Kalena's fever continued to climb. She lost nine pounds in four days. The hospital staff decided to pack her body in ice in an attempt to break her fever, which by now has reached 105. I was informed that if her fever reaches 107, her kidneys and other organs would begin to shut down. Lora and Stacey were with me at the hospital. We helped the nurses pack the ice bags around Kalena. The ice bags were around her head and neck, under her arms and down her sides, between and down her legs, and on the outside of her legs too and her feet. She was crying frantically and begging me to help her. I told her that we were trying to help her. I explained that we had to get her fever down, which was why she was packed in ice. She then said, "You're killing me, Momma. You're killing me. I'm going to freeze to death." She just didn't understand that we were trying to save her life. I was so enraged with that doctors attitude toward me and the way he talked to me or not talk to me. I began to make arrangements to have Kalena transferred to the children's hospital in Kansas City. I ran into the doctor one last time in the hallway, and again I asked him what he thought was wrong with my daughter. He told me that I wouldn't understand. I just completely lost control. I grabbed the knot of his necktie and the collar of his shirt and slammed him up against the wall. I commenced to tell him that I had spent half my life in a hospital. I could read and understand most of a patient's chart. I told him that my physical disability didn't have any bearing on my capabilities of understanding what was wrong with my child, and if he didn't start talking to me and telling me what he thought was wrong with my child, I was going to beat the hell out of him right then and there. Then and only then did he begin to tell to me that he believed that she had caught the foreign strain of flu that was sweeping the country and taking the lives of children and older folks around the country, and if we couldn't get her fever broke, she would be one of those children. I didn't know what I would do without Lora and Stacey there with me to support me. I said a quick prayer to God not to let my child die. When I finally got back into Kalena's room, I found out that her fever had finally broken and that she was going to be all right, so I canceled the transfer to Children's Mercy. Before her fever was finally broke, it topped out at 106.7. She came so close to the 107 mark and organ failure; I'd never heard of a fever that high before in my life. I had one very sick little girl, but now she was on the mend and going to be just fine. She's been out of school for about two weeks but would be returning in a few days. I never wanted to see her sick like that ever again. That was almost more than I could handle.

As time went on, I began to meet some of David and Stacey's friends from the city. These were friends whom they grew up with from childhood. First, there was Marq. They called him "Nigger" Marq because he was black, but I didn't like that word, so I just called him Marq or Big Marq. Marq was six feet and six inches tall and probably weighed about 350 pounds. He was a huge man but a very gentle giant. He loved women, and I mean *all* women. He said he hadn't met a woman he didn't like. He (Marq) also had a live-in girlfriend named J. She seemed nice enough too. The next friend of theirs I met was Ronnie. He was a nice guy from a rough home life and had been in some serious fights in his day. He didn't take any crap from anyone; he has a brother named Adrian, who was the same way. With the two of them together or separate, I would definitely not want to be any man on the receiving end of either or both of them when they were angry. They definitely didn't play around. They both, however, were very lovable and friendly toward me. As time went on, they accepted me into their lives as if they'd known me forever. All of us including their Kansas City friends got together from time to time and party on a weekend. I really enjoyed life with all these people. I truly felt included into their lives. They wanted only the best for me and my daughter, and I could feel that. They had literally become family to me and me to them. All of our kids were literally growing up together, David and Stacey's boys, Lora's kids, and my daughter. Kalena and Lora butted heads a lot. Kalena did not like Lora or her parenting skills and refused to be around her. I am not really sure Lora liked Kalena either. I definitely ran interference between the two.

One day, out of the blue, my baby brother David called me and told me he was coming to see me for a while. He's coming by bus, so my friend David and I went to the Kansas City bus station to pick him up. Little did I know that my brother David's visit would end my friendship with Lora. She crossed a line that, in my opinion, should *never* have been crossed. She did it with no conscience at all. The moment she laid eyes on my brother, she said she had to have him. She informed me the she wanted to f——k him and was going to f——k him, and there wasn't anything I could do to stop her. She'd always been that way. When she saw a man she wanted to f——k, she just simply went after him and got him. She had no regrets about any of them. I asked her *not* to do that to my brother, but she wanted what she wanted and to hell with the consequences, and everyone could be damned. Now I knew that my brother was also to blame because he allowed this to happen; he said he's on vacation and gonna enjoy himself. I wouldn't have been bothered at all had he been with someone that I did not know, but with her of all people, I just couldn't stand it. After my brother went back home, I couldn't stop thinking about the line Lora crossed, and I was filled with anger and hatred toward her. I decided that I'd got to do something to get back at her for disrespecting me and our friendship. I decided that I was going to go to her house. My friend David said he'd drive me there. When we got to her house, he wouldn't let me get out of the car. He did donuts in her yard with my car and then lofted a beer bottle at the huge picture window on the front of the house. It did not break the window, and I was really pissed about that. She wasn't home of course, and that made me mad too. I wanted to confront her and basically kick her ass. She avoided me like the plague after that. She knew that I didn't play around and that going to jail did not scare me. Now whenever I wanted to go to David and Stacey's house, I gotta make sure that Lora wasn't there, because I absolutely refused to be around her. David and Stacey were still friends with her and tried to get me to reconcile with her, but I refused. The only thing I would reconcile to was to hate her for life, and if given a chance to, I'd kick her ass one day. All I could say was that I hope she enjoyed my brother, because she'd *never* have him again, and she just lost one of the best friends she ever had because at one point I would have done just about anything for her and her kids and pretty much did too.

One day, out of the blue, after few months had gone by, my brother David called me and told me he wanted to move back here and live with me until he could get out on his own and said he needed to come home. He told me that he wanted me to come and get him and his stuff and bring him home. He sent me gas money for the trip and told me to find someone to ride along with me. The only person available to go with me was Marq. My only concern for this trip was driving down through the Deep South where prejudices still lingered. Here I was a white woman with a very large black man sitting in front with me traveling together. I wondered if we would encounter any trouble whenever we stopped for gas and such. Well, I just couldn't think about that then, because I had to go get my brother. Marq and I set out on a January morning just ahead of an ice storm. We were driving to Tallahassee, Florida, where we would be meeting my brother. We had only enough money for gas and a little food. We would be sleeping in my vehicle, which was an '87 Chevy Blazer. As we were driving through Arkansas, we came upon a fog so thick you could hardly see the hood of my Blazer. As I was driving along and I was only going about ten to fifteen miles per hour, Marq said not to stop and just keep moving. I couldn't even pull over, because I couldn't even see the shoulder. I was basically just inching along. Marq said if I stopped, someone could rear-end me, so I just kept moving slowly. The fog lingered on and on and on for hundreds of miles. We drove in fog most of that day even though it did get thinner as the day went on but never completely lifted. I'd driven in a lot of fog in my life but *never* anything like that. I was a huge Alabama fan (the singing group). I'd brought some of their CDs with me and told Marq that while going through the state of Alabama, it's only fitting that we listen to them through the entire state, and he agreed. I'd barely been out of Kansas and Missouri my whole life, so it was a trip of a lifetime for me. Even though we really couldn't stop and do any sightseeing because we were on a timetable, I was still excited and taking in all that I could see as we traveled along. We only stopped for gas and bathroom breaks, but so far we had not encountered any hostility anywhere. I was certainly glad about that. In fact, everyone we'd encountered had been extremely friendly toward us, and even helpful when necessary. We only stopped one time in a roadside area for truckers to get a few hours of sleep before heading on to Florida. When we left Butler, Missouri, everything was brown and dormant because it's wintertime, but when we entered the state of Florida, *everything* was green. I'd never seen anything like it. Green was everywhere. I saw that mossy-looking stuff hanging from trees. I'd only seen that stuff on TV. Everything looked so neat and *green*. All I could say was *wow*. I was in total awe of the sights. I felt I couldn't take it all in fast enough. I had to take some of this mossy stuff home with me to Missouri. Just wish I could see the ocean, but we were not going down into Florida but just at the top of the state. We found the place that we were to meet up with David at. He's there with his buddy waiting on us. He actually lived in St. Petersburg but had a buddy of his drive him and all his belongings up to Tallahassee where we met up with them. We only stayed long enough for David to load all of what he owned on the inside of and on top of my Blazer. He said his farewells, and then we were off and on the road again. When I mentioned that I wished I could've seen the ocean, David said we'd go a different route home from where we came. So we ended up driving along Interstate or Highway 10, whichever it was, and I got to see the ocean, even though we didn't stop I got to see it anyway. As we turned and headed north, I mentioned again that there was absolutely no way that I was going to go through Tennessee twice and not stop in Memphis to see Elvis

Presley's Graceland. I knew we couldn't stop on our way to Florida, because we were on a time schedule, but now that we were on our way home, there wasn't a time schedule we needed to adhere to. Marq and David had *no* choice or *say* in this matter, because I was stopping, if only for a short while, but they didn't mind, and I was glad. After parking across the street from Graceland and walking across the street, I noticed that Graceland seemed smaller than I expected it to be. The wall out front had been written on and signed by all the fans who had visited. We stood there and literally read the wall. I inquired about a tour of Graceland and was told that the cost was $18.95. We didn't have the funds for that. The only money we had left was for gas to get us back home to Butler, Missouri. David said he wished he had an extra $20 for me to take the tour, but he just didn't, and neither did Marq or me. Oh, well, maybe another time. I took lots of pictures of the wall and the house and gates and of course of me in front of them also. I, at least, had some proof that I was there. While the gates of Graceland were open, I did walk a few feet up the driveway and touched the grass and a nearby tree before a guard in the guardhouse politely asked me to come back to the gate. I thanked him for allowing me that much. I promised myself that if I ever traveled through or near Memphis again, I would tour Graceland even though I was sure the price would be much higher next time. But at least I could say I was there, touched the gate and everything, and saw it from the sidewalk. That was a thrill that I would never forget. By the time we arrived back in Butler, Missouri, safe and sound, Marq and I had spent fifty-two hours driving there and back in my Blazer. Wow, what a helluva trip!

Once again, David settled back into my home. He knew that he had to find a job as soon as he could. One day, a young girl I knew named Connie stopped by my house to say hello and visit me for a bit. She's a teenager of about seventeen years. When my brother walked in and saw her, he had an instant attraction to her. I introduced them, and shortly thereafter she left. After a while, David got a job working at Sonic as a cook. It's a job, and it paid. Plus, he also found out the Connie worked there too as a carhop. Connie had a boyfriend, but David said he wouldn't interfere with them, but he and Connie became good friends and hung out together a lot. He told me that he told her that someday she would be his—that when the time was right, they'd be a couple. "Whatever," I told him. "She is too young for you."

One day, out of the blue, the phone rang, and when I answered it, it was George. He told me that he and his wife were divorced and that he would like to see me if I was interested. Yes, I was interested, I told him. We began to see each other regularly. He seemed to be trying too hard with me for some reason. Something was different with him, or maybe it's me; I didn't know what it was. He kept offering to give Kalena money or things that she wanted. I stepped in and had to tell him to stop. She got mad at me, but oh well. He seemed to be trying to buy her affection, and she liked it, but I didn't. David and Stacey seemed to like George and the fact that I had someone in my life. He seemed to like them too. We all hung out a lot together, having cookouts and partying. I was not sure what George would think when he found out that I smoked marijuana. I'd never told him nor been around him when I was high. *Would he think less of me or maybe not want to see me anymore? Would this be a deal breaker for us?* I wondered constantly about it. Then, one day, I was with my group of friends and him when some joints (marijuana) got lit up and started going around. When one of them reached me, I took it and hit on it, right in front of George. I told him that I liked smoking pot and asked him if he wanted a hit. He said no, but what I did was my business, and he didn't have a problem with it. He did tell me that he was surprised that I smoked it, though. I was really glad to know that that didn't end our relationship. One night while George and I were out at Pizza Hut for dinner, I got a call that David had been arrested. George and I left the restaurant, and George went to pay David's bail so he could get out of jail. To me, this was very embarrassing, but it was what it was. One night, while George was at work, I just happened to stop by his work, and while I was there, his ex-wife drove up, and he went out to talk to her. I could hear her yelling at him about how our relationship, his and mine, was going to come to an end and that she was going to put a stop to it, that she was not going to allow her children to get close to me. When she left and George came back inside, I asked him how he thought she was going to end our relationship. He said that he didn't know but that he didn't think she was going to do anything. It's getting close to Christmas, and David and I decorated my whole house. We put up Christmas lights everywhere in my house, including on the ceiling going down my hallway. It literally looked like runway lights; it did look kind of funny but cool. When George brought his two youngest kids over, they were in awe of how everything looked, especially his daughter. She kept telling me how beautiful everything looked and how beautiful my house was. I must admit myself that everything did look pretty cool and that David and I did a pretty good job with all the lights and decorations. About a week before Christmas, George insisted on giving me my gift. When I opened the gift, it was a Kansas City Chiefs coat. I was thrilled because I was a Chiefs fan, and now I had a Chiefs coat to go along with the many Chiefs shirts I had.

George invited me and David and Stacey to go to the riverboat casino in Kansas City. So on December 23, two days before Christmas, we all got up really early and went to the casinos. George paid for everything, including giving all of us forty dollars each to gamble with. There just happened to be a Chiefs game on TV that day, and we all wanted to get home in time to take naps and get together to watch the game later in the day. We all had a great time at the casino, and then about 10:30 a.m. or so, we headed for home. We all got home and went to our respective houses. George came to my house, and then his youngest son and my daughter asked to go to the skating rink to skate. George gave them both money to go and took them there. George and I were sitting down to relax for a while when the phone rang. His ex-wife was on the phone and asked to speak to him. He took the phone and stepped outside to talk to her. A few minutes later, he came back inside and told me that she was going stop by shortly. A little while later, Nancy (George's ex-wife) stopped by in her van in front of my house. George went out the door to the street directly in front of my house where she was parked. I watched out the window for a moment or two, then sat back down and continued watching TV. After about ten to fifteen minutes, George came back in the house, except he looked real strange. The man who walked out that door a few minutes ago was not the man who walked back in. He's very quiet, wouldn't talk. He even looked different somehow. I asked what happened out there, what was said, but he didn't respond to me. I told him that I was really tired and would go to lie down and take a nap. He told me that he needed to go to Walmart and get his mother a Christmas gift. "Okay," I told him, "take your time, and wake me when you get back." He left my house, for what would be the very last time. Sometime later, my brother David came into my room and woke me up to tell me that George was on the phone and wanted to talk to me. I told David to tell George that I'd talk to him later. David told me that he truly believed I needed to take this call. "Why?" I asked. David just handed me the phone and told me to talk to George. So when I got on the phone, David left my room and closed the door behind him. George then proceeded to tell me that he had to leave town, that he was headed north to Illinois. I said, "What were you talking about? You were going to Walmart to get a Christmas gift for your mother when you left my house. What is going on?" Now George could be quite the joker when he wanted to. I was thinking that that was what he was up to now. So I told him that I was tired and going to go back to sleep. He told me again that he was headed for Illinois. I told him to stop this bullshit and just come back to the house. Then all of a sudden I heard another voice in the background. I heard Nancy's voice. I again asked what's going on and why Nancy was there with him. I asked him why he had to leave town. The words that came out of his mouth next were shocking. He said "I just killed a man and I have to leave town." "No you did not" I said. Again he repeated himself, "I've just killed a man." Then I heard Nancy saying something in the background but couldn't make it out. Then he said that I needed to go and get his truck and bring it back to my house and keep it there. I asked him where the truck was, and he told me that it's at Nancy's place where he killed her husband. I proceeded to tell him that I didn't believe anything he's saying to me. He told me to go the skating rink and bring his son to my house and keep him there and tell him nothing. He again told me to go and get his truck. I told him that I couldn't do that, because his truck had a stick shift, and I couldn't drive a stick shift with one hand. He kept repeating to me that he killed a man, and I had to believe that. Then I heard Nancy tell him to hang up the phone, and the phone went dead. There I sat in my bed, and my head was just reeling from this phone call. I just didn't know what to believe. I got up and went into the living room where David was, and he asked me what that phone call was all about. I told him everything George said. David asked me if I believed any of it. I told him that I didn't know what to believe. David told me that while I was napping, he (David) called the house wanting a ride home from work and that George had wanted David to go with him on his errand, but that David was tired and said no. David said that we both knew that George was a practical joker and asked me if I thought this was one of his jokes. Again I didn't know. Eventually, David went to the skate rink and brought the kids back at home. George's son kept asking where his dad was. I kept telling him that his dad went Christmas shopping for his grandma and that I didn't know what time he would return. I never mentioned the phone call to him. The hours passed, and still no more word from George. I just didn't know what to do or even what to believe. About eight or nine that same night, I finally called George's oldest grown son TJ and told him about the phone call and that I hadn't heard anything from his dad since. I asked TJ if he thought the call could be for real.

He said that he would check things out and get back to me, and to just keep his brother until he got there. Later, there was a knock at my door, and it's the police wanting to talk to me about the phone call I got from George. TJ had already come and gotten his brother. I told the police everything about the day and the call. They informed me that a man, Nancy's husband, was found dead at her place and that because of the call to me from George admitting guilt and running that he probably did do it. They also informed me that George kidnapped his ex-wife, which I didn't believe. They also told me that I would probably be subpoenaed for a trial. I was so in a state of shock right then. I didn't know what to think, how to think, what to feel, or even how to feel. Never in all my born days would I had ever thought that I'd go through something like this. The Police told me that it was a good thing that I didn't go and get George's truck. They also said that I could have been an Accessory after the fact, tampering with evidence at a crime scene, and possibly other things. I could not even begin to imagine what my mind would have done had I went out there to get the truck and actually saw that dead man and all the blood. This was something I was not sure how to handle or how to deal with. This was such a small town, and everybody knew George and knew me and knew we were seeing each other. What was this going to do to my daughter, not to mention his kids? After the police left, David kept asking me if I was all right. "Yes," I told him, "I am fine." He said, "No, you're not. When all of this really hits you, you're going to lose it big-time." No, I told him, I was fine, I was okay, but I could sure stand to get high right now; so I did, just to help me relax and calm down a little bit from all that's happened that day. I just couldn't seem to absorb all of this. I felt like I was in some kind of dream world, or maybe I should say nightmare? The next morning when I got up, I realized right away that yesterday was not just a dream. It really happened. George killed a man and then called and told me that he did. What kind of person does that? Not just kill someone but call his girlfriend and tell her that he did. None of this made any sense. Then all of a sudden I remembered the night at his work a couple of weeks or so ago. Nancy said she would see to it that his and my relationship would end, that her children would *not* be a part of my life. Well, it's done; she had made sure of that. I didn't know how she did it, but I believed she was somehow behind all of that or at the very least involved in some way. She was not the kind of person to make a threat and not follow through with it somehow. People in this town told me in the past that she was not to be messed with; some had even told me that she could be dangerous. She was behind that, and I knew it in my core but just couldn't prove it. Eventually, I told the police who also said that they believed she was somehow involved, but there was no evidence to prove it. I wanted to know what was said during that conversation in front of my house. The George who went out to talk to her was *not* the same George who walked back in. The physical body was the same, but the George I knew was not there. I had to talk to George and try to find out what happened that day to cause all of this; I really wanted to know on one hand but did not want to know on the other hand. Also I thought, *Do I and could I believe whatever he told me?*

David and Stacey were in shock over this too—said they couldn't believe that George did this and that they themselves saw no signs of anything like this coming. My brother David was hovering around me and wouldn't let me out of his sight. He said when it finally hit me, and that it would hit me eventually, he intended to be there with me and for me. I kept telling him I was fine, I was good. He kept telling me that that would change; he just didn't know when. On Christmas Eve, my brother David made me open his gift to me. It's a garage door opener. I really loved it. I'd had to manually open my garage door all the years that I'd lived here—pull into the driveway, put car in park, get out of car, get out the key to the lock, unlock the lock, turn the handle and raise the door, then get back into the car, put car in drive and pull into garage, put the car back into park, turn off key, and get out again. I had to do all those steps in reverse to leave also. Such a hassle, but I had been doing it for years in every kind of weather. I was so happy to have an automatic garage door opener. Both Davids together put the garage door opener on my garage door. It took them several hours to do so, but when all was done, it worked *beautifully*. A day or two after Christmas, *it* hits me. Out of the clear blue, I just started sobbing. I cried so hard that I literally became a blubbering fool. Slobber was running out of my mouth, and I couldn't control my emotions. I was crying uncontrollably and shaking also. Brother came over to me and just sat and held me and wouldn't let me go. No words were spoken between us, just the boy I helped raise into a man, and now holding his sister in a way like I used to hold him. I never thought I would lose it like this. Didn't know where all that emotion came from. David just sat and held me for the longest time. When I was finally able to quit crying and get myself under control, I realized how grateful I was that David, my baby brother, was there for me. I still couldn't believe that he knew that that would happen when the timing was right.

As the days went by, I found out that George wanted me to come to the jail and see him. At first, I did not want to go, but I was talked into it by my brother and David and Stacey, if for no other reason than to get his side of the story as to what happened out there that day in front of my house with his ex and at his ex-wife's house, where the murder took place. So on visiting day, I went to the jail to see George. After going through a physical search and pat down for weapons and/or paraphernalia, I was escorted to the actual jail. George was on one side of the bars, and I was on the other side. He wanted to hold my hand through the bars. That really kind of creeped me out, knowing that those hands shot and killed a man, and now he wanted to tenderly hold my hand. He told me that he was really sorry for all of this. I told him that I had to asked what was said between him and his ex outside my house that afternoon. He told me that Nancy said that because her husband was a trucker, he and some of his trucker buddies were interested in their daughter, who was only fourteen years old, and that they couldn't wait to get a hold of her. He said that she said that all the men wanted the girl, and even her own husband, and that that enraged him so much that he totally lost control and went out there to kill the pervert. He said that no one was going to mess with his daughter or even talk about it and get away with it. George said that he only wanted to scare the man, but things got out of hand, and he ended up shooting the man in the head with an assault rifle. I later learned that he also put three or four more bullets into that man's butt. To me, that was just over-kill, and the fact that George put bullets into the man's butt was a sort of statement. I was not sure that I believe that story. I believe that if Nancy told him that story, it was made up by her for a number of reasons. This was just my opinion, but as more things came to light and more people who knew Nancy very well came and talked to me, I learned things that were shocking. I learned about the life insurance policies the man had for years that she had her husband transfer into her name not too long before he died. I learned about the huge life insurance policy the man had that his son from a previous marriage was the beneficiary on, and how she tried like hell to get a hold of that one because it was for $1 million. Townsfolk told me that Nancy was all about money. So they were not surprised that she tried to get all of his life insurance payouts. Townsfolk also believed she was somehow involved with her own husband's death as do I, but there was no way to prove it. I believe that she got her ex-husband to kill her current husband, for one, to end our relationship like she said she would a few weeks earlier, and, two, to collect huge sums of money from his life insurance policies and move on to her next target. This was just all my opinion, but it's also a lot of other people's opinion in this town too. I also learned that it was Nancy who insisted that George call me that day and that it was her idea for me to go and get his truck and bring it to my house, but she forgot that I couldn't drive a stick shift. I just believe that she was hoping I'd ended up in jail too as an accessory of some sort.

As time went on, I got subpoenaed to testify for the prosecution in his trial. At another visit to George in jail, he asked me to marry him; he said that I'd get $300 a month from his disability and that if we're married I couldn't testify against him. "Absolutely not," I told him. Then he told me that he wanted me to have power of attorney to take care of his bills and his house. He told me to have all his utilities shut off, then to sell his house. He said his house was a little messy, but he did not prepare me for what I was to find at his house. When I unlocked the door and stepped inside, I was in shock at the sight. Stacey was with me, and we both just backed out of the house. I'd seen cleaner landfills. I'd never seen such filth in my life. A little messy didn't even make a slight dent into what that house looked like. The smell was almost overpowering. There was animal feces and urine everywhere; cobwebs, and cockroaches both dead and live ones were everywhere. There was so much trash everywhere, rotten moldy food. I thought, *How in the hell does someone live like this, or even live in this?* No wonder his kids liked coming to my house. This house didn't just get this way since he and his ex split; you could tell it'd been this way for years. There was a room in the back of the house that had trash in bags piled halfway to the ceiling. Some of the bags have been ripped open, and you could see moldy diapers and food and crap. Can't understand why the bags of trash weren't put out for the trash men to collect. Why would someone just fill up a room with bags of trash and not throw them out? David and David told me and Stacey that we're not allowed back in there. They themselves got duct tape and wrapped it around their pant legs and shirt sleeves and wore masks and rubber gloves before entering the house. They searched for anything salvageable. They found a few things. There was an upright freezer and bookcases and blankets and a few other odds and ends that they removed from the house. They took the freezer to the carwash and cleaned it there, and the blankets were taken to the laundry mat and washed there. The bookcases were cleaned in my driveway. As far as I was concerned, the house needs burned to the ground. The floors were all rotted and falling in; the furnace was falling through the floor, as was the toilet. I just didn't believe that anyone would want to buy this house. It's absolutely horrible and should be burned to the ground. A young man whom I knew remembered what the house looked like inside when he was a kid and wanted to buy it and restore it to its former glory. He checked it out and said the structure was in good condition and that it just needed to be gutted down to the frame and rebuilt. I gave him the price, and he offered a lower price, and I stood firm with my price, which he accepted and paid. I took care of all George's expenses and final billings and closing costs and whatever else with the money; then I kept the rest for myself. George asked me to put $1,000 on his account at the jail, but my brother David and David and Stacey convinced me to keep what's left for all the pain and suffering I'd gone through because of all this. After all was said and done, months had gone by, and I told George that I was done with him, and I was not coming up to see him anymore and for him not to contact me either, not now not ever. I told him, "Do not call, do not write, and do not send anyone to my house." He agreed to completely leave me alone and understood that we were through. I was not going to be the bride of a prisoner who'd be spending the rest of his days behind bars, and besides that, I didn't even know who he was and not sure if I ever did, and I didn't even like him anymore anyway. It's just not going to happen. My life seemed to be in quite a mess then. I just didn't know how I got myself into that kind of crap. I'd decided that I was done with men. I really didn't even like them at all anymore.

The last three men in my life were horrible choices. My husband was an alcoholic; the next guy was Greg, another alcoholic; and, finally, George, a murderer. Yep, I was definitely done. I decided to just keep men at arm's length from then on.

I couldn't even escape this crap at work; my customers were constantly asking me questions about George, like I really wanted to discuss him or anything about him. I did find out that my ex-friend Lora came to my defense. She worked as a waitress at a local restaurant, and some of her customers made comments that maybe I was somehow involved or that maybe I had some prior knowledge of what George was planning to do that fateful day. She squelched that nonsense. She defended me to all those people and let them know that I would never have been involved in any such thing or have any prior knowledge of such a thing. I had a newfound respect for her now. She could have thrown me under the bus, so to speak, but she didn't. I may not like her much, but I respected her for defending me when she didn't have to. I was so sick and tired of people asking me about George. I'd talked about getting a T-shirt that said "I didn't f——g know, and I didn't f——g care" when it came to George. I then found out that his family—his mom, brothers, cousins, and such—were blaming me for all of this. I just didn't get how they thought this was my fault. I did not kill anybody; *he* did. I didn't tell him to do. I didn't even know about it until afterward. I guess that they had to lash out and blame someone, so it's me. I could only imagine what my dad's wife, Betty, would think of all this. She'd have a field day with this information. This was definitely something she must never find out about my life, not that she ever would, since we didn't speak. I just know that Betty would so have fun with this information.

One day while at work, a customer walked up to me and asked me how George was doing. Something inside of me just snapped. I politely took care of the customer, and then I turned around clocked out and just walked out right in the middle of my shift. Not a word to no one, I just quit and walked out. I just couldn't take it anymore, customers constantly asking me about him, how he's doing, if he was okay, how they felt so sorry for him. I guess they just didn't think about what all of this did to me or what I was going through or how I was doing. When I pulled out of the parking lot, I headed straight to the Super 8 Motel, which was where Stacey worked. When I located her, she asked me why I was not at work, and I just completely lost it. I started crying and shaking uncontrollably. She kept asking me what's wrong, and it took me a minute before I was able to stop crying enough to tell her that I just walked out on my job. She said that she's surprised that I lasted as long as I did. I felt as if everything was out of control in my life. I thought, *How did I got myself into this mess? How do I pick up the pieces and move on? I can't, not as long as I am still connected to all of this, and the connection won't be broken until after the trial and this nightmare ends.* I'd been subpoenaed to testify at his trial as a key witness. I was so not looking forward to this trial. I'd never been a witness in a trial before. This was all new territory for me. When the day of the trial finally came, I wanted to be in the courtroom during Nancy's testimony, but I was not allowed in there until after mine was over. I was so curious about her version of the story because I knew that she would lie on the witness stand. That's who she was and what she'd do. The attorneys asked me before I was called in if I was all right and told me to just tell what I knew about the day in question. Then I got called into the courtroom and sworn in. Now getting sworn in was funny to me. They asked you to place your right hand, which I didn't have, on a Bible and raise your left hand and "swear to tell the truth, the whole truth, and nothing but the truth." All I could do was just raise my left hand into the air and swear the truth; it was accepted by the judge. Surprisingly enough, though, I was not at all nervous like I thought I would be. I answered all the questions asked of me and told what I knew of that day, and then I was excused. I knew by my testimony that I had just sealed George's fate. I was truly hoping this would be the end of all this mess for me. I just wanted to put all of this behind me now and move on with my life. I felt like I'd been in a very dark place for a very long time now. I wanted to see some light up ahead at the end of this long dark tunnel that I'd been in for so long. I just didn't want to think about this anymore.

Months went by, and I was feeling like I was moving ahead slowly but surely when, all of a sudden out of the blue, I got a phone call that George's lawyers were fighting for an appeal for him and wanted me to testify *again*. They contacted David and Stacey about me, and David and Stacey called me and told me what their intentions were. I went off, telling David that I would leave town, which he relayed to them. Then they said they would have me subpoenaed, and I said only if you could find me, and I began packing our bags as I was talking on the phone and was going to be in the car as soon as I hung up the phone. I didn't know where I would go, but my daughter and I would be gone within an hour or so. Then I proceeded to tell them that even if by some slim chance they could get me on the witness stand, I would either clam up and not say a word at all, or I would be an extremely hostile witness who would be absolutely *no* help to them at all, or worse. "Trust me," I told them, "I will not go through any of that ever again." They decided against it and told David and Stacey that they would never bother me again—a message that was passed on to me; and I never heard from them again. Well, that made me feel better knowing that I was able to control that situation, but I meant every word I said.

Well, at that moment, that was all behind me, whatever that was, and I wondered how long before I could feel normal again. I found myself smoking more and more cigarettes and *pot*! I just didn't want to feel anything anymore. I still went thru the motions of daily life. I still have a daughter to raise up and bills to pay and a home to take care of and a yard to mow and all the other things in my life. I was all my daughter had, and she depended on me, and I could not and would not ever let her down, and besides that, she was all I had too. I just felt like I was in a very dark place, and I didn't know how to get out of it. I couldn't let her know. I had to appear to be strong and in control. I was up to smoking about three packs of cigs a day and a whole lot of pot. I was glad that I was not a drinker anymore. If I were, I just might have been in trouble. I thought it's just going to take time and a lot of it before I could truly put all of this behind me and for people to stop asking me about him.

Months went by, and things seemed to be a little better, and Christmas was approaching. Since I had direct deposit of my Social Security disability checks, whenever the third of a month came around, I wrote out all the checks for my bills and put them in the mail on the fourth of the month. Well, it's December, and I did my usual routine with checks and bills. Then, one day, Stacey said, "Let's go Christmas shopping." We stopped at the bank so I could get some cash out, only to find out that I was overdrawn in my account. "That's not possible," I told them. I might get down to just a few dollars left in my account, but I was never overdrawn. "So how is that possible?" I asked them—like they were going to be able to give me an answer. They checked, and to all our surprise, my SS check was never deposited into my account at all. They also told me that I'd racked up a hefty amount of overdraft charges so far. I was totally stunned and didn't know what to do. I'd gotten more checks out there that would be coming in and making the overdraft charges even higher, not to mention the charges I'd incurred from the businesses that the checks were written to. My heart has just sunk again. How much more could a person (me) take? The bank offered me their phone to call the Social Security Administration to try and find out where my check was and why it wasn't deposited into my bank account. Much to my surprise, I was informed that I made more than I was allowed to make while working at Hardees Restaurant. So now they have stopped my checks until they recouped the money I was overpaid by them while I worked (*part-time*). The bank apologized to me and said that there was nothing they could do to help me. I left the bank to go home, feeling totally defeated and ruined. I was going to end up homeless with nothing. How in the hell do I fight the government? I couldn't fight them and win. No one wins against the government, no one. All I wanted to do now was just get high and get numb. I didn't want to feel anything anymore. My daughter would not have a Christmas that year, and I thought we may end up homeless. *Why does this crap keep happening to me?* I asked. I couldn't catch a break. This definitely was not living; I just seemed to exist in life. I was so angry at that moment, but I didn't know what to do then. David and Stacey were at my house with me and told me that I'd always have a place at their house if necessary. I appreciated that, but I just couldn't think about anything right now. I walked into my kitchen to be alone in my anger and washed some dishes. While I was in there washing the dishes, this rush of peace from out of nowhere came over me, and all of a sudden, I got this weird feeling that everything would be all right. Wow, what the hell just happened to me? I walked out of the kitchen and into the living room, and David looked at me and asked me what happened. I looked at him and Stacey and told them that I knew that everything would be all right. They asked me how I knew that. I told them that I didn't know how I knew this, but that an overwhelming sense of peace just came over me while in the kitchen. They told me that they could see it on my face. Then they asked me what I was going to do. "I don't know," I said, "but tomorrow I'd begin the fight. Right now, though, I am going to finish washing my dishes and then spend the evening getting high and watching TV." The next day, I got on the phone again and called the 800 number to the Social Security office. I explained the entire situation to the person I was speaking with. The person said to me that they were very sorry but that there wasn't anything that could be done. I would not be receiving my check for at least another five months. I hung up the phone in complete disgust. I waited a little while and called the number again. Because it's an 800 number, I got a different person each time and a different state too. I, again, went through the entire story, but to no avail. I just wanted to give up, but something inside of me just wouldn't let me. I didn't know what it was or where it's coming from, but I just couldn't give up, even against all odds. I called Social Security every day and went through the story and got nowhere. One lady even went so far as to tell me that I should contact the local church's in my area to help me out because they like to help people, especially at Christmastime. I thought, *Why won't these people at Social Security listen to me?* They were so coldhearted and unfeeling. They really didn't seem to care, and even talked to me like I was some kind of criminal; but something inside of me just wouldn't let me give up. I didn't know what it was. I'd never had a feeling like this before. On about the fifth day of calling, I got a hold of a gentleman who actually *listened* to me. After hearing my story, he said he's not sure what he could do to help me but that he would try. No one had said those words to me before. All I'd heard all week was, "Sorry, I can't help you," "Sorry, I can't help you," "Sorry, I can't help you." It was the first time somebody was telling me that they're at least going to try. I had hope for the first time all week. The man put me on hold and, a few minutes later, got back on and asked me how much could I afford for them (Social Security) to take out of my check each month until all the overpayment was returned? We agreed on ten dollars a month, and he told me that he would have my Social Security check deposited into my bank account before the end of the day. "*Great*, oh, wait a minute," I said to him. I told him that as soon as the check hits the bank, all of the overdraft charges would eat up a significant amount of the money. All of the checks I wrote to pay my bills were now coming thru the bank and bouncing left and right. He told me that he didn't know how to help me with that. I suggested that he call my bank and explain to them that because they (Social Security) withheld my check and, thru no fault of my own, the overdraft charges were made. I told him that maybe he could ask the bank to waive the overdraft charges this one time, especially since my bank records would show that I *never* wrote bad checks. He agreed to do that, and I gave him my bank's phone number. A few minutes later, he called me back and said the bank agreed to waive all the overdraft charges this one time. He said my check would be in the bank before the end of the day. I simply could not thank this man enough for what he did for me. I told him that I believed him to be an angel sent to help me and asked him what state he worked out of and his office address. Turned out he worked in the office in Kansas City, Missouri. I got his name and his supervisor's name and their office address and mailed a letter to them out of extreme gratitude. I praised him to his supervisor and explained everything to him and how he helped me when nobody else would. I learned a few lessons from this experience: (1) I'd never send out anymore checks in the future until I know for sure that my SS checks have been deposited into my account. I took it for granted that they would always be there because they always had been before. Never again. (2) Keep track of all my future earnings so I won't have this problem in the future. (3) Good things do happen in this world, and I believe in angels. Always did before but never experienced one until right then. This now explained that feeling I had about not giving up. I didn't know why I had to wait a week for the help, but it's done and right at Christmastime too. I did thank God for it, although I was not living a Christian lifestyle. I couldn't imagine why God would want to help me especially with the way my life was now. But just couldn't think about that anymore. I had more phone calls to make. I started calling all the businesses I wrote checks to and explained things to them. One by one, they all agreed to resend the checks back thru my bank, and they also agreed to waive the returned check charges, again because my records showed that I had never written bad checks before.

Well, time passed, and life went on, and things got back into a stable rhythm for me. I was a creature of habit and didn't much care for change. People say that they could set a clock to me, whatever that means. It's 2001 and David's mom, Terri, was not doing well, health wise. David and Stacey moved her in with them. The doctors had given her six months, and she had a DNR signed. It's May of that year, and one morning, I went over to the house, and when I walked in, I saw Terri in her wheelchair in the living room. I looked at her and instantly knew something was wrong. She was gray looking, and something was just not right with her. I truly didn't think she'd live out the day. A few hours later, she passed. I didn't know how I knew, but I just did. It's a very sad day for that family, especially David. He and his mom were very close. I believe it was going to be very hard for him, as well as for the rest of the family. She, Terri, did not make it the six months the doctors predicted.

My daughter graduated from high school that same month. Graduation day that year also happened to be on the same Sunday as Mother's Day. I told my daughter that she didn't have to get me anything this year for Mother's Day, because just watching her graduate and get her diploma was present enough for me. What better gift could I possibly get than to watch my girl graduate from high school? I couldn't think of a single thing. We'd gotten all the invitations sent out. I didn't know how many people would show up for her, but I'd definitely be there, along with my brother David and his girlfriend, Connie; Amy and Curtis; David and Stacey; and a few others. I wished my mom could be there to see it and wished my dad would come, but I knew it's not going to happen. A couple of hours before graduation time, there was a knock at my door, and when I opened the door, there stood Uncle Tom and Aunt Betty. They came for Kalena's graduation. I was shocked to see them but so glad they came. In a way, Aunt Betty was representing Mom, who was her sister, and Uncle Tom was representing Dad, who was his brother. I was sure they didn't see it like that, but I did. The graduation was in the high school gym. I was surrounded by my little group of people who have come to watch my girl graduate. The gym was literally a full house. The band began to play the "Pomp and Circumstance" song, and the march of the graduates into the gym began. I saw her, and, oh my gosh, I just couldn't believe my baby was graduating.

She's all grown-up, not really, though. She looked so cool in the cap and gown, which turned out to be not her gown. When her cap and gown came in, the gown had all these creases in it that Stacey decided it needed to be ironed. So she ironed it and scorched a huge iron print on the back of it. Stacey freaked out and apologized over and over and didn't want Kalena to know what had happened. We scrambled to find one we could borrow from a former graduate. We found one, and Kalena would never know that it's not the one she ordered and received, and then afterward when she thought I'd put all of it away, I'd return it to the owner, and Kalena would be none the wiser. As the graduation continued and all the speeches were done with, an announcement was made, asking that all the applause be held until all the seniors had received their diplomas. They said that they didn't want people clapping and yelling after each person went across the stage, for people to wait until the last one exited the stage; then we the audience could give all the seniors one collective applause. I'd got news for them: that was *not* going to happen. I decided that when they call my daughter's name, Kalena Elizabeth Taylor, I am going to stand up and yell, and I could pretty much guarantee that those who were with me would do the same thing without any prompting from me. That was just one rule I would not abide by, not on this particular day. As the names were read and each one went across the stage, the gym was mostly quite. Once in a while, someone's family member would give a shout out or a small clap. When Kalena was next in line for her name to be called, I got ready. Then the announcer said, "Kalena Elizabeth Taylor." The group with me and I stood up and exploded into yelling and cheering and clapping. I was so very proud of my girl, and although we probably just embarrassed the crap out of her, I thought deep down she knew it was going to happen, and she probably liked it. After that, other people began clapping and shouting for their graduates. I guess someone had to break the silence, and we certainly did that. I didn't care, and besides no one is going to tell me that I couldn't cheer my daughter at her graduation, and, yes, afterward, the whole place erupted into applause for all the seniors as well. What a milestone for her, and she was still only seventeen, and won't turn eighteen for another month. I was one very proud mama that day.

When she turned eighteen, she got a little stupid, and I took her car keys from her and told her that she was grounded from driving until further notice. She was very angry at me but did not challenge me. I knew that I didn't have any right to take her keys and keep her from driving since she was eighteen and of legal age now. She bought the car she had herself with all the money she got as graduation gifts, but she would not challenge me at all. A few weeks later, her dad called out of the blue and wanted her to come and see him because she was eighteen. I believe he was living in Tennessee then. She told him that she couldn't. He asked her if she had a car, and she told him yes. He proceeded to tell her how to drive there. She then told him that she was grounded from driving and that I took her car keys. He told her that I had no right to ground her or keep her keys, because of the fact that she was eighteen and legal. He told her to demand her car keys back and to come to see him. He had no idea of the relationship that she and I have. Even though she was eighteen, I still controlled her and would continue to do so for as long as I can. I knew that one day soon that would all change, but it's not that day. She later came and told me about their conversation and how he told her to demand her keys back so she could come see him. I asked her right then point-blank, "Are you challenging me on this?" She answered, "No, ma'am," and went on about her way. She might be eighteen, but she was still just a kid who needed guidance. Being eighteen doesn't make you an adult mentally or emotionally, only physically and legally. I still had a job ahead of me, helping and hopefully teaching her how to navigate some of adulthood before she's ready to try and tackle it on her own.

August was here, and a group of us had decided to go on another "canoe float trip." David and Stacey and their boys, my brother David and Connie, Kalena and I, and a few others made plans to go. Kalena asked if we could take our dog Suka with us, and I said, of course, we could, especially since all the ones who could care for her were going on the trip. Not quite sure how well she (the dog) would do in a canoe, but I thought we'd soon find out. We were so excited and couldn't wait. Our kids had not gone before, so this should be fun. We explained to the kids that before anyone could go swimming or wandering off to explore, we must first set up the campsite and gather wood for the bonfire. Absolutely everyone helped getting the campsite set up, including getting tents all put up. We all helped each other getting everything set up so that we could all enjoy the time together as a group; no one was left to fend for themselves. Well, the weekend arrived, and everything went as planned. Camp got set up, firewood was gathered, and a bonfire was built. The adults partied into the night. Early the next morning, we went down to the river where our canoes were waiting. We loaded up with our coolers full of beverages and of course our delicious Jell-O shots and our lunch and snacks, and started off down the river. Everyone was having a great time, and kids were loving this too, even our dog Suka seemed to be enjoying the canoe ride, although she jumped out of the canoe once and went straight under the water and my brother David had to pull her up and put her back into the canoe. We spent the entire day floating down the river and just having a great time and enjoying each other's company. Later that evening back at camp, everyone was just exhausted from the day and drained from the sun. Most of us took naps before fixing dinner. We again party into the night, not looking forward to packing up in the morning for the long trip back home. Morning did come, and we tore down and packed up everything and headed for home. Once Kalena and I got home, I discovered the entire inside of our house was black. Black was everywhere, the walls, the ceiling; everything was black, and it's very warm in there. The air conditioner wasn't on. *What the hell happened here?* I thought. Kalena said it looked like it's been burned. She thought that someone must had broken into our house while we were gone and set it on fire. I checked the doors, and they were not broken into, and none of the windows were broken. She left to go get her uncle David and David and Stacey. They arrived and called the fire department, and I called my insurance agent. The fire chief said that it was definitely a fire and that it looked to had gotten pretty hot inside the house, approximately 2,500 degrees by the look of things. He said had we come home a day earlier and hit the garage door opener, it might have blown us across the street. He also said that because my house was so airtight, the fire smothered itself out after a while, and no one ever knew it was even on fire. I lived in a raised ranch house, and nothing in the basement was damaged. Only the upper part of the house sustained fire and smoke damage. We discovered that the fire was caused by a cigarette. David and Stacey offered us a place to stay in their home till we could figure out what to do. Kalena, however, stayed at our friends Amy and Curtis's house, which was just two blocks from David and Stacey's. I'd never dealt with anything like this before. My insurance agent walked me through everything. He was a great help to me, and I really appreciated it. I continued to stay at David and Stacey's house while Kalena stayed up the street while our home was redone. Insurance gave me an allowance for rent, and I split it between David and Stacey and Amy and Curtis for allowing each of us to stay in their homes. The contractor hired to redo the house said it may take approximately four months to get the job done—that we should be able to move back in before Christmas. On the morning of September 11, Stacey was at work, and David and I were drinking coffee and watching *Good Morning America* with Diane Sawyer and Charles Gibson when the one of the World Trade Center towers was hit by plane. Then we saw the second tower got hit live on the air. Then whole country was thrown into total chaos.

David and I were in total shock, as was everyone else. We were completely glued to the TV, wanting more information as to what was going on. As the day wore on and it's discovered that this was an act of terrorism, I didn't understand this. *What does that mean? Are we no longer safe in this country?* I was not sure how to feel or what to do. As the days went by and I saw people buying and hanging the American flag everywhere, I felt and understand for the first time in my life what patriotism means. I'd never known this feeling before, but I liked it, and I liked this country. Something I guess I took for granted until now. This really put things into perspective for me.

Amy came to me one day and told me that they're having some issues with Kalena. Well, I couldn't have that. So I talked to her uncle David who worked as a delivery driver for our local bakery. He left at about three or four in the morning and delivered all over the place, like up in Kansas City, Missouri, and over into Kansas and even down south. I told him that I wanted Kalena to go with him, and I wanted him to work her ass off. She was not just going to sleep all day at Amy's house and stay up all night and do absolutely nothing. I had an extremely long talk with her, and explained that she was a guest in someone's home and was to act accordingly. She was to help out at every turn. I explained that they did not have to put up with her and that she needed to show gratitude for their hospitality. I also explained that while she was learning that lesson, she would be accompanying her uncle David on his delivery runs every morning at about 3:00 a.m. It's not up for debate, and she had no choice in that matter even if I had to get her up myself. She protested, but she went with her uncle David. After a few days, Amy told me that whatever I said or did had made a difference in Kalena, she was being helpful and respectful.

After several weeks of staying with others, Kalena and I needed a break too. I contacted the insurance agent and explained that we needed to get away for a few days. I explained that, although we were grateful for the people we were staying with, we needed a break from them as much as they probably needed a break from us. The insurance agent cut us a check for a trip out of town. Kalena and I took off to Springfield for a weekend and went to Fantastic Caverns.

I'd seen the commercials on TV for years and always wanted to go, and we did. It's really nice that Kalena and I could just go somewhere together and have fun. We had a great time on our getaway.

Back in Butler, the contractor had me go and pick out all kinds of things for my house. I got to pick out vinyl flooring, countertops, paint, carpeting, kitchen and bath fixtures, lighting fixtures, etc... I'd never done anything like that in my entire life. Never realized how many choices there were. One thing was definitely for sure: I would never smoke in my house again or allow anyone else to smoke in my house either. My home would be a smoke-free home from then on. I hoped it would help me to cut back on the amount of cigarettes I smoke, because I could smoke upward of three packs a day. The remodel of my house was coming along nicely. After the entire inside of my house was gutted down to the studs and insulation, the contractor set off a special bomb of some kind to rid my house of the smoke smell, and even put something into the ductwork to do the same. I had to stay out of the house for at least twenty-four to thirty-six hours while the bombs did their work. He said afterward no one would ever be able to smell the smoke or be able to tell there had ever been a fire.

I went over to my house at least two to three times a week just to check on the progress. I couldn't wait to get back into my own home again. It's nice to stay with friends, and I was really grateful they had taken us into their homes, but there truly is no place like home. It's the first part of December, and we finally got to move back home. I was so very excited! Everything was so fresh and clean and new. I couldn't wait to celebrate Christmas this year. It had been one helluva year for me.

Time went by and life went on, and everything was back on track as it should be. It's April of 2004, and as I had always done, I went over to David and Stacey one day, and as I was walking up the front porch steps, David began to yell at me to go home. He yelled for me to get the f——k off his property. I continued up to the door, wondering where it was coming from. I was just over there yesterday, and everything was fine. Stacey told David to stop it, that it's just me. He continued to yell obscenities at me, demanding that I get the f——k off his property and never come back. Stacey came to the door and said she didn't know what was up with him and asked me to just leave so he would calm down. She said he'd probably be all right by tomorrow. Well, the next day came, and David was still the same. For some reason unknown to me, I was no longer welcome in his house or his life. I had known them and been their best friend for more than twelve years. We had been closer than some families. I'd been like a sister to both of them, an aunt to their boys. I didn't understand what had happened. Why had David turned on me like that? Stacey continued to come over and visit with me and hang out, but her visits were becoming fewer and fewer. She had a trip planned in August to visit her father in Arkansas. When she came back from that trip, she never spoke to me again. I felt totally lost without them in my life. Then over time some of the townspeople, one by one, started coming up to me and telling me things about David—things I never knew, things he had done to some of the people in town, the lies he had told, the cons he had pulled off, the things he had stolen. The kicker was when his best friend told me that David had told him that he (David) and I had slept together. That was why his best friend's wife hated me, and I never knew why then. Now it all made sense to me. She hated me because she thought I was sleeping with Stacey's husband all the while being her friend. Why would David make up such a lie like that? I informed his best friend that that was a lie, completely not true; it never happened. The friend said that he believed me. His friend said it was because that's just how David was, that he always wanted what he couldn't have and would tell certain people that he had or got *it*, whatever *it* was. It just made me sick that David even thought that way about me. I still didn't understand why Stacey turned on me, though. I knew a lot of people in this town, but they were my best friends, and now I didn't have anybody to hang with. I thought I'd just stick close to home now. I was working part-time at our local McDonald's, so I'd just go to work and home. The roommate I had named Alan who rented my spare bedroom said that he saw things in and about David but knew I wouldn't have believed them if he had told me. When I asked why, he said that I had blinders on when it came to David. Other people had said the same things to me about David. I just didn't want to think about this anymore.

One day, out of the blue, I got a letter from the government agency that I had my house through, and the letter informed me that *all* persons in my house must report their income to the agency. This angered me because my roommate just rented a room from me—that's all. He (Alan) bought his own food that was separate from mine. His income and debts were none of my business, but the government agency informed me that I could be fined, imprisoned, or both, and could lose my house too. So after I showed the letter to Alan, I asked him to find another place to live, because I would not lose my house for any man. He understood, and after a couple weeks, he moved out. I felt I could never get ahead. I'd like a roommate because it would help me out financially, but I was not allowed that. If I reported a roommate, then they (the government agency) wanted that person's monthly income so they could *max* out my house payment, when in fact that person's income was not a part of me or my household income. Well, I just couldn't think about that anymore. I'd got to make some changes in my life. I was so tired of things as they were. I just didn't know what to do or even where to begin. I felt as if something had got to give in my life. It's July of 2005, and I decided I was giving up smoking pot. I wanted to quit smoking cigarettes too, but I was going to take things one at a time. I smoked the last of pot that I had and get rid of all the smoking materials and pipes and paraphernalia that I had. For some unknown reason, I felt the need to get myself into a church. I had no idea where that came from, and I had no idea what church to go to. The only churches I'd attended in years had been for weddings and funerals. I grew up in a Christian church, so I thought I'd start there. I got out my phone book and looked up Christian churches. I found one there in town and drove by to see its exact location and time of service. I couldn't believe that I was actually thinking about going to church. I almost felt like I might be struck by lightning or something if I entered a church for myself and not for a wedding or funeral. It seemed the only time I'd even went to God in prayer was in bad or troubled times. I knew enough about God to know that he wanted me there and would forgive me if I just asked, but I didn't really feel like I had the right to ask anything from him with the life I'd led. I mean I'd broken almost all of the ten commandments in the Bible. I was not sure I'd forgive myself if I were God. I guess it's a good thing that I was not God. Well, I finally got up the courage to get up one Sunday and get myself together and go to church. When I walked into the church sanctuary and sat in the back and looked around, I saw dozens of people I knew. A lot of the people I saw were customers and former customers of mine from Hardees and McDonald's. It's a small town, so I thought I'd know people in any church I'd walk into here. I truly never thought about that. I was kind of hoping no one would know me and I would not know anyone. People start coming up to me and welcoming me and hugging me. Then one of my older lady customers named Lilah got up from her seat, grabbed her things, and came and sat next to me. I was truly impressed by that act of kindness. I learned that the church didn't have a regular minister, but they had what was called an interim minister named Dr. Dave Corder for the time being. He was amazing, and I really liked him. I also discovered that nothing bad happened like lightning striking or something because I was in a church. Well, I continued going to this church every Sunday, one, because I wanted to and, two, because I felt welcome and comfortable. Well, a couple of months had gone by, and I got the news that David and Stacey's niece Kelly had passed away. I was very sad, and my heart was heavy over this news. That beautiful blond-haired blue-eyed little girl was gone. I just couldn't believe that. I kept remembering when she yelled out to me to get my attention by calling me "Broken-arm Lady." I definitely wanted to attend her service but was not sure if I should, because David and I we're no longer friends, so I was not sure if I would even be allowed. I didn't know what David had told his sister Denise about me. I didn't know if Denise would even want me there. I decided to call Denise myself and extended my sympathy to her and asked if it would be all right for Kalena and me to attend Kelly's service. Denise said we absolutely could come and were very much welcome. She said that Kelly loved us and that Kelly referred to me as an aunt and family. I was so glad to hear this. I so very much wanted to say goodbye to that beautiful girl. Upon arriving, I discovered just how many people's lives that very young girl touched. The place was packed with people just to say goodbye to her. One person was missing, though. David, her uncle, was not there. I couldn't imagine why he wouldn't be there for his sister Denise and to say one last goodbye to his niece Kelly, whom I knew he adored. I just hope he didn't stay away because I wanted to attend. On the way home from the services, I was offered some pot, but I said *no* to it without hesitation. Wow, I could hardly believe I said no. That was huge for me then because I had loved getting high daily for years. I guess I just grew bored with it, but something was definitely happening inside of me, not quite sure where it was coming from or why, but I thought I'd go with it and just see where it went.

I discovered that I actually enjoyed going to church. I didn't attend any Sunday school yet—just church service. The church I was attending had two services. The first service started at 8:30 a.m. and was called the contemporary service, with Sunday school after that, then the late service called traditional following, at about 11:00 a.m. I did not want to get up too early, so I attended the late service. Besides, I liked the traditional service, because they sang the old gospel hymns I grew up singing, and there was nothing in the world like those old hymns. Those old songs reminded me of my childhood, listening to my mom, grandma, and aunt Betty singing them in church and at home.

The year had finally come to a close, and I thought that next year I would try to quit smoking cigarettes. I was down from three packs a day before the fire in my house to about a pack a day and sometimes less, so I hoped quitting wouldn't be so hard. McDonald's had asked me to come in and start working on Sundays. They wanted me to work the drive-thru window. Until that point, I never gave a second thought to working on Sundays or any day for that matter. At that point in time, all I wanted to do was attend church on Sundays. I told the boss that I'd only come in and work after church. Service was over at 12:00 p.m., and I'd be in shortly thereafter. The boss was all right with that. Wow, I couldn't believe I just stood my ground where church was concerned. I really didn't have to fight for it, because I was firm about it. I couldn't imagine where all of that was coming from. My daughter's father, Rick, had reentered the picture after all these years. I thought he'd be ready to be a dad again, now that she was grown. He wanted her to come and live with him in Georgia. She wanted to go. She wanted to get to know him. We discussed it, and she decided to do it. He was an over-the-road truck driver, so he said he would come to Butler and pick her up. When he finally got here, I was shocked at his appearance. He looked so frail and thin. Those were two words that just didn't go together when it came to describing him. He was a fraction of the man I used to know. Everything in me told me that there was something very wrong with him. I didn't say anything to him about his appearance. I invited him to go with Kalena and me to one of our local restaurants for dinner. Rick and I hadn't seen or been around each other since 1992, when I kicked him out of our lives. After we had our dinner, we sat and really began to talk. Kalena was sitting next to her dad as we were in a booth. Rick and I began to reminisce about the past. We keep saying, "Remember this," or "Remember that." We both began to laugh almost uncontrollably. I noticed that Kalena was really enjoying seeing her parents together and getting along and laughing. She was so very young when I kicked him out. Whatever she remembered, if anything, of us together was probably yelling and/or fighting. We sat in that restaurant for over three hours, talking and laughing. That was a memory I would always cherish giving to our daughter. She just got to spend an evening with her parents where there was joy, laughter, and a great time had by all. I never thought I could be around that man without spewing venom and angry words. I truly know and believe it was a God thing. The next morning, they got all her stuff loaded up into his rig. We took some pictures together and said our goodbyes, and off they went. I still couldn't get over how badly Rick looked. Something was definitely wrong with him, but I was really glad that he and Kalena had this time to get to know each other. I was going to quit smoking, and I had purchased several items to aid me in this. I bought the pills and the gum. After a week or so, the pills didn't seem to be working. Next, I tried the gum, and that stuff was nasty tasting. I tried and tried and tried to quit but couldn't seem to get past a week. I kept telling myself that if I could just get past the first two weeks, or the first month; then I'd have it licked. In the meantime, Kalena called me every single day and had since the day she left with her dad. I thought she just needed to hear her momma's voice. She asked me if I missed her yet. I told her that I couldn't miss her when she's calling every day, but, yes, I did very much. I finally broke down and bought the "stop smoking" patches, which to me were kind of expensive. They seemed to work better than anything else I'd tried so far. I just kept thinking, though, if I could just get that first month or so under my belt that I'd be smoke free. It just didn't work for me. I kept trying to quit but couldn't. I just didn't know what to do. I was totally at a loss for ideas on how to quit. I'd heard stories of people who asked God for help with alcoholism, drug addiction, and other things; and God cured them instantly. They said that there weren't any lingering aftereffects or withdrawals or cravings or anything. That's what I wanted—just be cigarette-free without withdrawals or cravings. I'd tried all year to quit, and nothing worked for me. It's the end of another year, and I was still smoking cigarettes. The year 2007 was a couple of days away. Three months after that, I would turn fifty, and I wanted so badly to be cigarette-free before I turned fifty. I kept thinking about those stories of instant healing from addictions. As midnight got closer, and 2007 was a short while away, it dawned on me that I'd been going about quitting all wrong. I'd been thinking how to get past the first week or two, or first month, and then I realized that tomorrow is not promised to anyone. Yesterday is gone, and all we have is today. Then the song by Cristy Lane, I believe, "One Day at a Time" popped in my head. I had to literally take things a day at a time. I finally got it. It's almost midnight, and I dropped to my knees and asked for God's help to quit smoking cigarettes. I asked God to please keep the withdrawals and cravings away, and if *he* won't do that, then to at least make them tolerable for me. I don't believe in New Year's resolutions, because people do not keep them. I would not do this as a New Year's resolution; I just wanted to quit at a time that would be easy for me to keep track of. The first of a month, that just happened to be the first of a new year. After my prayer to God for his help, I destroyed and threw out what cigarettes I had left and then went to bed. When I awoke the next morning to a brand-new day and year, I asked God to give me the strength to just get through the day. I did, however, put on one of those "stop smoking" patches. The day went very well. I had a couple of cravings, but they were very mild, and passed quickly. When I went to bed that night, I thanked God for his help getting through day 1 and praised him. When I awoke to day 2, I again asked for God's strength to get through the day; he gave it to me. Again, at the end of day 2, I thanked God and praised him. The days turned into a week, then two weeks. I continued to pray each morning for his strength, and prayer of thanks and praise at the end of each day. A month had gone by, and I realized a couple of things: one was that I had forgotten to put the patches on. I thought that with God's strength I didn't need the patches; and the second thing I realized was that I quit smoking one day at a time. Then at the end of February, I started having severe pains in my abdomen and discovered that my appendix was about to burst. I ended up in a hospital in Kansas City for an appendectomy. All went well. With that, and a couple of weeks later, when my fiftieth birthday rolled around, I believed I started becoming a nonsmoker. I did not want to ever start smoking again like some people do, so I asked God to make cigarettes and smoking completely repulsive to me. I wanted to start getting myself healthy. I didn't take very good care of myself most of my adult life, so I thought I should start. I quit smoking pot and cigarettes, and then I decided to work on my foul language, which wasn't as bad as it was. I discovered that being around people who smoke really stank. I couldn't believe I used to smell like that. I had to wash all my clothing to get the smell of cigarette smoke out of everything. I couldn't stand to be around people now who smoke. They absolutely smelled so badly, and I didn't even realize it. Months had gone by, and I thought I could officially consider myself a nonsmoker. It was so great, and God was so great. I just couldn't thank him enough for helping me. I realized that I couldn't do it on my own, but with God's help, I did do it. I would still continue to take things one day at a time and praising God at the end of each day. I was totally amazed at how things were going in my life at that moment. The feeling of accomplishment I had inside just over quitting smoking cigarettes—that was something I *never* thought I would ever do. I always believed I would smoke my entire life. I had heard people talk about how God took away bad things in their lives when they asked for his help, and I could say then that I was one of those people. I was totally blown away by this fact. There's a line in a song that was sung each week at church that I really concentrated with all the emotion I had, and it almost always moved me to tears. The line was "Praise God from whom all blessings flow..." I heard that song many years ago, but the words were just words to a song and did not register in my mind like they do today. God was definitely blessing me, and I was praising him. Kalena continued to call me every day. She said her dad had been going to a lot of doctor appointments. Then she called and told me that her dad had cancer. I was totally not surprised because of the way he looked when I last saw him. I just knew something wasn't right with him. He was so thin and frail looking. She's definitely not getting along with his current wife, Sherry. His marriage to that woman was not legal, because we were never divorced. I told him that, and I told her that too. He told me that he told her that he sent me money to get a divorce. That was a lie. He told me that it satisfied her, and that was all he cared about. Rick and I talked a lot over the next few months. He called me whenever Sherry left the house. He was no longer able to drive truck because of his health. While talking one day, Rick told me that he took 100 percent of the responsibility of the breakdown of our marriage and apologized to me. I so very much wanted to let him have all 100 percent of the responsibility, but as I was growing in my faith, I couldn't do it, because it takes two. He told me in our conversations that he was still in love with me and always would be. I didn't know what to say to that, because I did not share that same feeling. I had grown to care about him now. All the hatred and anger and bitterness I had toward him were now gone, and that also surprised me. With God's help, I'd forgiven Rick. Kalena stayed for almost a year with her dad and simply couldn't take her so-called stepmother any longer and came home. I was glad to have her home. The last time I spoke to Rick was on Thanksgiving Day. His speech was very garbled and difficult to understand. A couple of days or so later, we got a call from one of their neighbors whom Kalena had become friends with that Rick had passed away. I myself was in total shock. I always believed Rick would outlive everybody because he was just too mean to die. I couldn't believe I was crying over his death. I was really surprised at these emotions where he was concerned. I hadn't been around that man in seventeen years until he picked up our daughter last year. Would God's wonders never cease?

My coworkers at work were telling me that I was different. I found myself talking about God at work to my coworkers. I'd never done that before anywhere, and I was all right with it. I was truly not bothered by it. I felt this desire inside of me to talk about God to anyone who would listen to me. I didn't know a lot about how everything works with God, but I knew I could tell people what God did for me. I learned that there was a Bible study group on Wednesday evenings at the church, so I decided to go and check it out. Well, as it turned out, I knew mostly everyone there, and my neighbor up the street from me was the leader of the class. I started going to this class every week. I wanted to surround myself with Godly Christian people. I knew that being around other Christian people would help me to stay focused on God. I was discovering that I liked going to church because I wanted to, instead of being made to go like I was as a child or being made to feel guilty if I didn't by others. I never wanted to sit in church feeling like a hypocrite, or pretending to be something I wasn't. I started to go because I felt drawn there, drawn to God. I wanted to learn about God, his word and how he works. I was still in shock as to this turn around in my life. Not sure where it came from, but I decided to go with it and see where it leads me.

I contacted my sister Kim occasionally over the years and spoke briefly each time. I wished we could develop a relationship. We were friendly on the phone and the rare occasion we saw each other at the folks. I did get to go to my dad's house. Betty lifted the ban from that, I guess because we were all getting older now. I figured I could tolerate her for a short time in order to see my dad once in a while. I understand that the Bible said that you have to forgive others, because you yourself had been forgiven. I was having a very hard time with that where Betty was concerned. She had done me and especially my brother David *wrong* so much in our life. I just didn't know how to let go of these feelings toward her. I kept replaying this phrase over and over in my head: "The unwillingness to forgive is like drinking poison yourself and expecting the other person to die." I'd also been told that hanging onto this anger and bitterness was allowing her to win." I just couldn't or maybe won't let go of it. I felt if I let it go, then I would somehow disrespect my mom and her memory. I also understand that "forgiveness" is for me and not for the other person. I also know that forgiving someone is not a get-out-of-jail-free card. It did not erase what they did or said. Forgiving someone is for you yourself to have peace. I understand all of this, but I'm just not able to do it yet.

One day, out of the blue, my sister Kim called me, and we began talking. We talked like we never had before. It was so wonderful to talk to her. She and I began calling each other constantly. She informed me that her church was planning a mission trip to the Dominican Republic to help with the building of a church and to help spread God's word. She asked me if I'd like to go with her and the group from her church. Wow, a mission trip; how awesome would that be? She told me that I would need a passport. I'd barely been out of Kansas and Missouri, and I was excited at the prospect of being able to leave the country. I told her, *yes*, I'd love to go if I could raise the money necessary to go. She told me to raise approximately $1,000 to $1,500 for the trip. Some of the money had to be paid in advanced increments. A coworker of mine from McDonald's named Genna told me to try and raise approximately $2,000 for unforeseen expenses. She had traveled abroad before. Another coworker named Meghan told me that she would use her computer skills to design a flyer that I could put up around town asking for donations. I also went to my church and told them of the upcoming mission trip and explained that I would need all the assistance in raising the funds to go. I had about eight or so months to do this and had the absolute confidence that I could do this. I talked to all my customers, and one by one, they began donating money to my trip. Meghan got the flyer finished and made several copies, and I took them around town and put them everywhere. I went to all the local businesses and told them about the upcoming mission trip, and most of the businesses donated money. I kept track of every name or business that donated to this trip. I wanted to be able to send out thank-you cards to each person and/or business that contributed. I told people that no amount was too small. Some donated as little as a dollar. I was extremely grateful for any amount because it got me just that much closer to my goal. I spoke with my sister weekly on the phone and sometimes on speaker phone in meetings with the group from her church in Oklahoma. I could feel my faith growing inside of me. This was such a great feeling. This town of Butler had really rallied around me to help me go on the mission trip. I was so impressed with the people of my town. During some of the phone conversations with the group from Kim's church, I learned things about traveling to another country—things I never knew or would even think of. They said to *not* drink the water at all and not to eat any food that might be offered by the locals, even though they mean well. They told us that all our food and water would be provided for us. We're told never to leave the compound where we would be staying without one or more persons with us, and that they preferred that we went out in groups. I learned that there was a shortage of electricity on the island, and it went out for hours sometimes. We were not to bring or wear flashy jewelry of any kind. The females must bring and wear dresses when attending any church services—the whole "when in Rome" thing I guess. I'd had to buy one since I didn't own a dress and hadn't in years. I just couldn't believe this opportunity that had come into my life. Never in a gazillion years would I ever have thought that I would go on a mission trip and for God no less. I truly loved the closeness that Kim and I had developed. I just know that it would last too. I was very anxious to meet all the people that would be going, and they, too, were anxious to meet me.

As the months went by, I'd realized my financial goal for the trip. Boy, the people, my customers, businesses, and my church in Butler really came through for me. I just couldn't thank them enough for all their help. God had shown me just how awesome he was by providing a way for me to go on this trip. I knew if he didn't want me to go, then I would not have gone. We were given a list of things to bring on the trip, and I had everything I was supposed to have. I received my passport; and that was so cool to me, especially since I'd never had one, or even seen one. I truly hoped and prayed that I would be able to use this passport many, many times in the years ahead. I wanted to fill it up with stamps from all over the world, God willing of course. The day we would be leaving for our trip would be my fiftieth birthday. What an absolutely awesome birthday present. The day I turned fifty, I'd be on my way on a mission trip to "share" God's word with others. I couldn't think of a better gift than that.

The day had arrived, March 13, 2007, when we all met in Wichita, Kansas, at the airport in the wee hours of the morning. There were about twenty-three or so of us. We met and greeted each other and boarded the airplane and flew to Atlanta, Georgia, then laid over there for a while, then flew onto Santo Domingo, which was the capital of the Dominican Republic. From there, we took a bus ride about three hours inland to a poor small village where we would be working. The compound where we were staying was big and beautiful. It looked like a tropical island, which it kind of is. The backyard of the compound was full of banana trees and a type of palm trees. I didn't have words to describe this beauty. I'd only seen this kind of scenery on TV. One thing I did notice was that there was trash everywhere. I thought people just threw everything on the ground. I'd never seen such a trashy place, beautiful but trashy. The language was Spanish, which I didn't speak. The missionaries who lived there were the interpreters for us, and the locals. There were several teenagers who came on the trip from Oklahoma, one being my sisters' youngest son named Cody. Cody was sixteen and a very beautiful young man with a heart of gold. He had become quite protective of me and looked after and helped me whenever he could; he seemed to keep an eye on me all the time. I learned that I would be helping the ladies with Vacation Bible School. We're going to be teaching the local children about Jesus. I also helped to make lunches for our group with food provided for us. I knew this time was going to fly by very quickly, and I wanted to take it all in or as much as I could. I had a camera and was constantly taking pictures of everything and everyone. The locals had not seen anyone with an artificial leg before. They had missing limbs from whatever happened but no prosthetics. They either hopped around or were carried. They stared at my artificial leg, especially the little children. I sat down in a chair and took my leg off and let them look at it up close. They held it and passed it around. They were fascinated by it. I had never ever done that before. I'd never in my life taken my leg off around or in front of strangers, ever. For some reason, I was completely comfortable doing this, which was a first for me. I knew this was God. After a while, some of the elders of the little community called the children away from me and wouldn't let them be around me anymore. I tried to tell them that it was all right and that it wasn't a bother, but they were very adamant about keeping the children away from me. I couldn't understand why. No matter how hard I tried to tell them it was all right, they kept shooing me away from them. I felt like I had done something wrong, but I didn't know what. I later learned that it was all because of the tattoo I had on my ankle. I had a tattoo of a butterfly, and in their culture, tattooed people were drug runners or associated with drug runners. I had to get our missionary interpreters to explain to the elders of the community that tattoos in America were strictly an art form and nothing more. Once the elders understood this, they allowed the children to be around me. Boy, I never realized how different cultures could be. I just couldn't believe that a tattoo could cause such uproar, but it sure did. Although we adults had problems communicating with the locals, I'd noticed that our teens and the local teens seemed to be able to communicate just fine even though there was a language barrier. They all played together in basketball daily. It's so fun to watch them together. During one of our VBS days with the young children, we handed out baggies to all the children; and inside each baggie was a little plastic cross, some string, and colored beads. All of which were to be made into a necklace. We were told that only the children could have them because we didn't have enough for the adults. We were to make sure each child got a baggie. Our leaders began demonstrating how to put it all together, exactly which colored bead to put on and in which order because the order of color had significance, and then the cross and more beads. As I was walking around checking each child's progress, I came across an older woman with one of the crosses on the string. She had put it around her neck and was holding the cross tightly with her hand. She had her eyes closed, and I assumed she was praying. I couldn't understand her, because she was speaking Spanish, but I did understand two words: "Jesus Christ." As I watched her, I noticed she was clinching that little purple plastic cross as if her life depended on it. Then, all of a sudden, it hit me: her life really did depend on that cross, her spiritual life anyway. I began to cry almost uncontrollably at the revelation. I didn't think I'd ever seen anything more beautiful and moving in my life. If I see or learn nothing else during this trip, what I just witnessed was worth the entire trip. Nothing had ever moved me so much in my life as witnessing that woman and a little purple plastic cross. There was no way I could take it from her or ask her to give it to one of the children. I would literally fight anyone who would even attempt to do so. I went on this mission trip to help teach people about Jesus and to hopefully make a difference in people's lives, and I was the one who was learning and being taught. I was just amazed at how all of this made me feel. I was feeling things I'd never felt before. I felt a sense of true compassion for the likes of which I'd never known. I found myself wanting to do more of this kind of thing. I didn't necessarily want to be a missionary, but would like to travel and help out with mission work.

When our time there was coming to a close, I found myself not wanting to leave. I was truly enjoying this mission trip, or maybe I was enjoying more all the learning I was getting. These people had truly changed my attitude and even some of my life. I'd never known anyone to had so little and yet be so happy. Back home in my country, one could never have enough. It seemed that the more one has, the less happy and/or content they are, so they strive to get more. In the Dominican Republic, they do not have and couldn't miss what they've never had. We could all learn from them.

The day we arrived back in Wichita, Dad, Betty, and my other family members were there to greet us at the airport. Betty was genuinely excited to see us, even me. She came up to me and gave me a big hug and told me that she's glad we made it back safely. For the first time, I actually feel her sincerity toward me. I was going to have lots of stories to tell of this trip for a long time. When I finally arrived back home in Butler, I went straight to my daughter's workplace, Sonic. When she saw me pull in and get out of my car, she came running out to greet me and literally picked me up off the ground in a huge bear hug. She was so afraid that I would never make it back alive and didn't want me leaving the country ever again.

My brother David became an over-the-road-truck driver. He called me almost daily to talk. We got into some pretty deep discussions about God and the Bible. One day, during one of our conversations, I mentioned tithing in church. I said that I put five dollars in the offering plate every now and then whenever I could afford it. David told me that we were supposed to give 10 percent of all our income to the Lord. He said that, somewhere in the Bible, but he couldn't remember where, it says if you're not tithing like God said, then you are robbing God. He also told me that God said you could test him on that. I told him that you were never to test God. I remember that from childhood, you were to *never* test God. David said that wherever the scripture was in the Bible, it's the only time you could actually test God. David said that God says, "Give what's mine, and I'd open the floodgates of heaven. Test me on this." Okay, now I was on a mission. I'd got to find where that scripture was and read it for myself. David couldn't remember where in the Bible it's at. He didn't even know if it was in the Old or New Testament. After days and days of searching, I finally found the scripture. The Bible verses are Malachi 3:8–10. In the NKJV, it says, "Will a man rob God? Yet you had robbed me! But you say, 'In what way had we robbed you'" (v8)? In tithes and offering, it says, "You were cursed with a curse, for you had robbed Me, Even this whole nation" (v9). "'Bring all the tithes into the storehouse, That there may be food in My house, And try Me now in this,' says the Lord of hosts, 'If I would not open for you the windows of heaven And pour out for you such blessing That there would not be room enough to receive it'" (v10).

Wow, I never knew that. I was robbing God every Sunday by not tithing and not tithing like I was supposed to. David said that Malachi was the only place in the entire Bible where God said, "Test me." When I knew that I could actually "test" God on this, I decided to do it. I admitted I was a little scared because 10 percent of my income was a lot of money to me. Just my Social Security alone, 10 percent would be $100. I kept thinking that I could do a lot with $100. It was where I decided to really put my faith to the test, as well as on God. I'd never in my life put my faith on God to the test. But here goes. When my SS came in, I took a $100 right off the top before paying anything else. Then at church, when the offering plate came by, I almost couldn't put it in the plate. I hold onto the envelope and heard this voice in my head, saying, *Trust me*, so I let go of the envelope into the offering plate. I said to myself, "Okay, God, I going to trust you. I can't wait to see what you're going to do." Well, the very next week after paying all my bills, the only cash I had left was a $100. That had to last me until I got my next paycheck from McDonald's, which, by the way, was small since I only worked for fifteen to twenty hours a week. It's springtime, and I had my riding lawn mower in the shop to be serviced. It always ran between $80 to $100, depending on what all needed to be done. I went into the shop and asked Kenny (the owner) what the damage (amount) was. He got this puzzled look on his face and seemed to be thinking for several seconds and then, out of the blue, looked at me and said, "I don't know why I'm saying this, but just give me forty dollars, and we'll call it good." You could've knocked me over with a feather. I was in shock, but I knew exactly why he was doing that. It was a *God* thing, and I had absolutely no doubt about it. I paid the man his forty dollars and left. I was just floating right now. I just experienced God acting on my behalf; I have no words to describe this feeling. I couldn't wait to see what's next. That experience just helped grow my faith. As I began to tithe 10 percent of all my income on a regular and consistent basis, I soon discovered that I was never broke, not rich in cash but never broke. My bills were all paid; I had gas in my car, food in my house, and a little extra spending money. I'd experienced many other financial blessing in my life since then. When I started to understand tithing, I have since decided to always tithe as God asks of me. I shared this news with David; he said it helped him in his faith too. We talked on the phone almost daily while he was driving over the road; he said he got bored driving, so he called people to talk to.

David stopped at my house once a month for a weekend to spend time with his kids at my house. Since his wife left him, that's the only time he got to see them. He and the children went to church with me whenever they're here. I'd been asked at church if I'd like to be a deacon. After some study and thought, I agreed to do so. Some of my duties as a deacon were to serve Communion occasionally on Sunday morning and to attend monthly board meetings, and also to be above reproach. I couldn't tell you the honor I felt when I got to serve Communion to my brother. I was so honored, and tried so hard not to cry, because it was very emotional for me. I held back the tears, but it was hard. David said he tithes also, but he sends his tithes back to a church in Virginia where he lived before driving truck.

A storm came through and really mutilated my roof. Insurance approved a new roof for me. David said that all I had to do was purchase the shingles, because he would put them on for me. That would save me a little extra dollars. In the fall of 2008, David came and spent the weekend, and I got a couple of male friends James Culpepper and Shain Burk to help, and for a thanks and payment, I fixed a huge dinner and fed everyone. Shortly after this, David found out that his kids were not in a good environment because their mother was making a lot of really bad choices. He went to court seeking custody of his children, and the judge said that he would grant custody only if he came off the road and got a different job and provided a stable environment. David asked me if he and the kids could live with me until he could get on his feet. Of course I said yes. He just had to find a job and a car and save money, and then get a place of their own. When he went to get the kids, we had to go to their school to get them. He had all the paperwork proving he had legal custody to pick them up. When we took the kids, all we took were just the kids. No extra nothing. All we had were the clothes on their backs. The hardest part of all this was having to leave Shaun behind. Shaun is not David's biological son, but David raised him since he was a year old, and he was about twelve years old at that time. David tried to explain to Shaun that the judge couldn't grant custody of him, because he is not adopted by David. David is the only daddy Shaun ever had, and he couldn't be with him or his siblings. I'd just gone from living alone to having three kids and my brother living with me for an indefinite period of time. My home was not set up for children. I didn't have any toys or games, or even clothes for the kids. I contacted some of the people from my church and told them the circumstances, and within hours, I had people dropping off clothes, some new and some used, for the kids. Their aunt Jennifer also brought some clothes for the kids. Just another show of God's blessings appearing. Within a few days, the kids had a few changes of clothing and some underwear and socks. David got the girls (Jasmine and Journey) enrolled in school. Vince was only three years old, so he was not in school. The kids seemed to be a bit withdrawn and skittish. They were definitely not their normal selves. I told David that in time when they see and realize that they are safe and secure and have a sense of normalcy, they would relax and be all right; kids are resilient. After a few weeks, we began to see the security in their actions and behavior. It's really great to see that. I was witnessing firsthand the effects of constant TV and video games on a child. That had been the life for Vince. He constantly wanted to watch TV or play video games. I told him no and to play outside. I got a few matchbox cars for him to play with on the driveway, and after fifteen minutes, he told me that he was done playing and was ready to watch TV. He didn't play at all; he just sat there and waited. I came to realize that he didn't really know how to play. All he had ever done in his three short years was watch TV and play video games. Well, I thought that would have to change. He and his sisters would have to play outside daily. I live across the street from a park, and they were going to be using it, just as my own child did.

As the days and weeks went by, David and I actually saw the kids begin to relax and stop being so uptight. We had them on a schedule daily, so they knew what to expect, and all was going well. I just wished Shaun could be there with us. Wherever he was, he was alone and missing his siblings, and they were missing him. Connie was keeping Shaun away from David just to hurt him. Once in a great while, she let Shaun call and talk to his brother and sisters, and if we're lucky, David got to talk to him too. Finally, after a few weeks, Connie let Shaun come for a visit. As soon as Shaun entered my house, he jumped into David's arms, and the two of them embraced for a good five minutes or more. Neither one wanted to let go of each other. Both were in tears, as well as me. That was a sight to behold. Although they were not biologically related, they were still father and son. That was a sight I would never forget as long as I live. Love is definitely thicker than blood in their case. I just wished Shaun could live with David permanently. We just had to settle for the occasional visits in the meantime. One day, while the kids were playing in my basement after dinner, I heard something break. It sounded like glass. I went to the basement to discover that while throwing a ball around, the oldest girl, Jasmine, broke a crock plate that I had on a table down there. I got so angry and began yelling at her. She ran upstairs and crouched down behind a living room chair scared. When I saw her there, I felt so bad for scaring her. We had gained so much ground with the kids, and I just blew it because of my anger. My brother told me that he would take care of everything and for me to go to my weekly Bible study group. So I left the house upset at myself and still a little angry because of the plate. Every week at Bible study, the leader (Alan) would ask each person how their week had gone. When he got to me and asked that question, I just lost it and broke down in tears. I thought everything was getting to me. I went from living alone one minute, to having my brother and three kids living with me the next. David was not making much money; and having four extra mouths to feed, more laundry to do, and my utilities also going up had taken their toll on me. David did what he could and helped out around the house. Money was just so tight then, and with Christmas coming, I didn't know how we were going to provide for the kids. After I composed myself, Alan led a prayer for me, and then everyone in my Bible study group started handing me money, ten-dollar and twenty-dollar bills. I tried not to accept it, but no one would hear of it. They insisted on me taking the money. Later that week, I received more money from different people who had heard of our/my plight. Even one of my other brothers (Joe) sent us some money to help with gifts for the kids. We were able to get each kid, and we had Shaun at Christmas (PTL), a bicycle, for a total of four of them, plus a few other things for Christmas. I, however, received the best gift of all that year. The grade school where the kids went had a little store, so the kids could buy things for their loved ones for real cheap prices. David had given Jasmine some money to get her brother and sister something for Christmas. She got them something, but she also got me something too. She felt bad for breaking that plate and wanted to replace it. I was totally unaware of this. The plate that she broke was a type of crock plate and had blue on it, and it was very old. The little school store had a blue plate for sale for a dollar, so she bought it for me. When she handed me a wrapped gift on Christmas day and said it was for me, I couldn't even imagine what it could be. David said when he helped her wrap it for me, it made him cry. Now I was really puzzled as to what it could possibly be. As I was opening the gift, I realized that I had a captive audience; then I saw the blue plate and realized what she had done, and I burst into tears, which, in turn, made everyone cry. She said that she knew it wasn't like the one that she broke, but it was about the same size and had blue on it, and as soon as she saw it, she knew she had to get it for me. No gift could or would ever mean more to me than that one because of the thought behind it from the innocence of a child. I decided to treasure that little blue plate for the rest of my life. It was one of the best Christmases ever, and God is great!

Over the next few months, David was able to save up enough money to be able to get a place of his own with the kids. He rented a house just across town from me. I was sure they all loved their house because everyone had different rooms. In my house, all of them shared one room because it was all I had. He had been seeing and spending time with a coworker of mine from McDonald's named Susan. Since I had my house back to myself, I loved the solitude. I still checked in on David and the kids regularly.

My entire family had decided to take a family vacation to Branson that summer of 2009. It was the first time we would all be together at one time in many years. My friend Laurie from Wisconsin helped my sister Kim and me to pay for our share of the condo rent because we couldn't otherwise afford the trip. God bless Laurie for that. She is definitely a blessing in my life in more ways than I can count. A few days prior to the trip, I took my car in to get it serviced—get oil and filter change—to make it ready for the trip. The day of the trip, David and I got our cars loaded with everything, and I even took two of his girls with me because he had no extra room in his car with all the supplies loaded in it. Off we went to Branson driving down Highway 13. About an hour into the trip, I noticed my car was smoking really badly, so badly that I had to pull over to the side of the road. David was ahead of me and saw the smoke rolling out from under my hood and stopped, pulled over, and backed up to me. I got the girls and myself out of the car. He jumped out of his car and came back to where we were and saw that we were safe. He popped the hood of my car, and the smoke was thick. A few minutes later, a white pickup truck pulled up behind my car, and a gentleman got out and walked up to us asking what had happened. He and my brother looked under my car, as well as under the hood. They discovered that I hadn't got any oil in my car at all. My engine was basically blown. The man explained that he left his house that morning from Nebraska headed for Branson and that the Lord told him to take Highway 13 because he was going to be needed later that day. He said that he argued with the Lord because he would never take Highway 13 otherwise. He said that the Lord was insistent, so he obeyed. A few hours later, he came across us, stranded. All of the stuff in my car would never have fit into my brother's car, plus three more people. The man offered to put everything from my car into the back of his truck and let the three of us (the two girls and myself) ride with him the rest of the way to Branson. We were very hesitant, but he kept reassuring us that we'd be okay. David said he would stay very close to us so as to not let us out of his sight, so off we went. This stranger literally drove us all the rest of the way to Branson, and right to the resort where our condos were, and even helped unload everything for us. He refused to take any money for his help or time. He just said that he was simply doing what the Lord had told him to do; he wished us all well and took off. Once again, God had shown himself to me. I called my daughter and told her about the car and where it was located. She contacted her boss who had a trailer, and he went and got the car and brought it back to town and dropped it off at a car repair place for inspection. After returning from a week in Branson with the help of David's girlfriend, Susan, who came to Branson a day or so before we were to return home and helped to bring us home, I discovered that the car engine was definitely blown. Apparently, when the oil was changed, the oil plug, which was only put in finger tight, vibrated loose, causing all the oil to leak out. The engine got so hot, and my gauges didn't work, so I never knew anything was wrong until smoke came rolling out of the car. By then it was too late. I fought the big retail store that serviced my car for months and months, but to no avail. All I wanted was $1,350 for the loss of my car, but their high-powered attorneys helped to keep them from paying me a single dime. I decided to not worry about this, because I had no doubt that God would provide a vehicle for me. He had proved himself over and over to me, so I decided to trust in that and just keep the faith. In the meantime, I got rides to work and got around town from various family and friends.

One day, I was in need of a haircut, and my regular hairdresser was no longer available, so I had to make an appointment with a place I'd never been before with someone I didn't know. On top of that, I didn't and couldn't get a ride, so when I called to cancel and explain why, the lady said she would come and get me and bring me to the shop. I couldn't believe she would do that for someone she didn't even know. While at the beauty shop, the only other person in the entire shop was a man sitting off in a chair reading a magazine. The lady named Pam and I got to talking, and I told her about the trip to Branson and everything that happened with my car, the stranger, etc... When she was done, she said she couldn't take me home but that the gentleman sitting there, who turned out to be her husband, would take me. Later that day, I got a phone call from Pam's husband. As it turned out, he had been listening to my conversation with his wife, and he was very good friends with the owner of the local car dealership Max Motors in town. He went to the dealership and told them about me and my situation and asked what they had in the way of something good and used. They had a 2000 Mercury Grand Marquis. It was in excellent condition, had new tires, and well maintained; and everything was in working order. It was supposed to sell for $2,300, but for me, they would sell for $800. He asked me to go and look at the car and test-drive it. So I did and even took my brother with me. After driving it, I took the car to a mechanic that I knew and had him go over the car and tell me if it was okay and worth the money. Curtis checked the car out, and even another mechanic checked out the car. Both of them test-drove it. They both told me to buy the car, and if I wouldn't, then they would. I took the car back to the dealership and asked if they would take payments. I told them that I could have that car paid for in about six to eight weeks. They said no, that I had to have all $800 up front. I didn't have $800; all I had was $350 and didn't know where I was going to get the rest of the money. They told me I have two weeks to come up with the rest, or the deal is off. I didn't know what to do or where to turn. I didn't know anyone with that kind of cash on hand to borrow from. I had a talk with God about this situation and decided to trust in him as usual. I thought if the car was meant for me, then the money would come. While at work one day, I discussed my situation with a coworker named Debbie. Out of the blue, she said she'd loan me the remainder of what I needed to get the car. In shock, I asked if she was serious. She said yes, and that she'd bring me a check the next day. The very next day, she handed me a check for $450. I took the check, cashed it, added my $350 to it, and went and bought the car. I would never in a million years have thought of my coworker Debbie to help me. I just couldn't thank her enough for what she did for me. I later found out that the husband of the lady who cut my hair decided to buy the car for me and to let me pay him once I get the money to pay for it. Within a month, I paid Debbie back, plus an extra $50 just because. I was learning so much about faith and trust in God. When I put him first in my life, he made my life easier. Thank you, Jesus.

I am learning more and more about the God I never knew about growing up. Growing up, I not only feared God but was afraid of God. I have finally (with God's help of course) found a way to forgive all the people in my life who have wronged and/or hurt me. I was able to forgive Rick (my husband), whom, for many years, I hated with a passion. When he learned he had cancer, he called me and apologized for the breakdown of our marriage and said that he took 100 percent of the responsibility for it. Since I have returned to my faith, I couldn't, in good conscience, let him take all the responsibility; after all, it takes two. We became friends after that. Even though each of us moved on with separate lives, we never divorced. He lived in Georgia, and I here in Missouri. He came to see our daughter, and the three of us went out for dinner and reminisced about our past life together. We laughed so much that evening, with the "do you remember this, or do you remember that." Kalena got to see her parents together laughing and having fun, which was something she never had growing up, and for that, I would always be grateful to God. When I told him that I am writing a book about my life and that he would be a part of it, he told me to be sure to tell the truth. I asked if he had his heart right with the Lord before he passed, and he said he did. I truly hope that is true. I just couldn't believe that when I got the news of his passing, I actually cried. He was a man I had grown to hate, and at one point, I even prayed for him to die. I really regret those feelings and prayer now. God was changing me on the inside, and I couldn't be happier about it.

As I continued to work at McDonald's, I was becoming increasingly unhappy with this job. I wanted so badly to just quit my job, sell my house, and move away from here. I'd actually put my house on the market a couple of times with absolutely no luck at all. I guess it's not meant to be right now. I did find myself talking about God and my faith to my coworkers and anyone else who would listen. I never would have done that a few short years ago. I told management at work that I won't work on Sunday mornings, because I went to church now, and that was very important to me. They scheduled me to come in after church and work afternoons on Sundays. I understood that God talked to everyone all the time but that most people didn't hear or listen, me included. I didn't know how to hear him. I knew that Betty's mother was not well. I always loved her mother. I knew I had forgiven Betty for the past, but I have never done anything for her. Betty had been going to her mother's house and spending time there with her brother Bill, helping to care for their mother.

One Sunday morning, while I was getting ready for church, I actually heard God tell my heart to go see Betty at her mother's house. I told God no, that I had to go to church and then to work. Again, God told me to go there. Again I said no, that I was going to church, then to work. Then, all of a sudden, I felt the prompting really strong telling me to go. So I told God that I would make plans to go another time soon. God said, *No, you'll go today.* Then I told God I would go to church, call into work, and go to grandma's house after church. God said, *No, you'll go now.* I have never felt such a prompting in my life, so I said, "Fine, I'll go now." I hadn't been to grandma's house since I was a teenager and didn't remember how to get there, and she lived in the country. I was sure the landscape had changed a lot in forty years. As I took off in the general direction for the hour and a half or so drive, I told God I didn't remember how to get there, so he would have to guide me. All the way there, I talked with God and felt prompting where to turn. Next thing I knew I saw her house and was pulling into the driveway. I drove right straight to the house without any wrong turns. No other explanation than God. When I got there and knocked on the door, Uncle Bill let me in. When Betty saw me, she was stunned. She asked me why I was there; I told her that I didn't know why except that God told me to come. She seemed genuinely pleased to see me. I spent the day there, visiting with her, Bill, and grandma. A few months later, grandma passed away.

I had reached the point of no return with McDonald's. I put in my notice to quit at the end of October 2010. I didn't just give them a two weeks' notice; I gave them a little over a months' notice. I was just really tired of working around food. I had been in the fast-food industry for over fifteen years, and I was done. It's definitely time to move on. I just was not sure which direction to take yet. I thought I was just going to take a break from working for a while. I was going to pray about it and see where God would lead me. That was something new for me, asking God's opinion about my life. I would ask him where I should go next; I always made my own choices before. Some of my coworkers had a party for me on my last day of work. Homemade food and desserts were brought in. That was really nice of them to do that for me. I really appreciated them all.

The year 2011 had arrived, and I was just living on my Social Security, less $100 a month in tithing. I was surviving on $900 a month and completely trusting in God for everything. I was able to pay all my bills each month, even though my utilities were kind of high. My house was all electric, so my electric bill was rather high in the winter. I had a couple of those Eden Pure heaters, and they helped a great deal. I could keep my thermostat lower and use the heaters for added warmth. I found that even as I was tithing a $100 a month and living on $900, I was never broke. I always had a little cash on me. When I wasn't tithing, I was always broke and *never* had any extra cash at all. It's strange that I actually gained more money when I started to understand tithing than I ever did before I tithed.

My brother Joe called me and wanted me to come and visit him and his family in Virginia this summer. I really wanted to do that. I'd never been to Virginia, and he had built for his family a log house that was my dream home too. I really wanted to see it and them. I just had to figure out to come up with the funds to get there and back. Joe said all I need was to get there. I'd be staying and eating with them, so there wouldn't be any charge. Flying would be easier for me because I wouldn't drive that far. Now to raise the money for a round-trip plane ticket. I decided to cancel my Dish TV service for a while, and I turned off my landline phone services too. I then began going through my house and cleaning out stuff. I decided to have a garage sale and raise money that way too. Whenever I had a garage sale, I also baked several batches of brownies the night before and wrapped them up individually and sold them. People *loved* my brownies, and they sold quickly. I enlisted the aid of my nieces to help with the garage sale. I ended up having three garage sales that spring and early summer. I had now saved up enough money and purchased my plane ticket, but I hadn't got any spending money at all. I made a decision to withhold a house payment to have some spending money while I was out there. I had absolutely no doubt that I could and would get it made up before the end of the year. After all, I'd had to withhold house payments in years past, and I always got it made back up, so I had no doubt that I could do it again. I completely trusted God and that everything would be all right. A friend and neighbor took me to the airport, and I flew out there. When I arrived at their house, it's dark, so I really couldn't see the outside of their log house, but the inside was beautiful. The next morning, I had coffee on their huge front porch surrounded by woods. This house and where they lived were absolutely breathtaking. I could completely understand why they called it their sanctuary. I thought someday I would have a log house of my own and live somewhere as beautiful as where they lived. I spent two glorious weeks with them and had a great time. During those two weeks, Joe, his wife, Tina, and I took a road trip to a resort hotel and an Amway convention. The hotel was something like off TV. It was so fancy, like for wealthy people. There was a doorman who greeted you as you pulled up, and even opened your car door and helped you out. I had never experienced anything like that. I'd only seen that done on TV. I met some of the most awesome people there that weekend. I even met the current reigning Miss America Teresa Scanlon of that year, even had my picture taken with her too. A great time was had by all. That trip was something I would never forget. I hated to come home, but all good things must come to an end. After arriving home, I decided that since I'd been unemployed for almost a year, it's time to look for another job. After all, I had a house payment to get made up before the end of the year. I started applying for jobs around town and nothing. I applied at a car dealership, Wal-Mart, and a few other places. After a while when I'd gotten no calls, I even went and reapplied at McDonald's. I *really* didn't want to go back there, but nothing else came along. I saw some of my former customers from McDs around town, and they told me that they missed me so much and that McDs was just not the same without me. That made me feel good. I was getting letters from the government agency that held the lien to my house, and they were hounding me for their money, and rightfully so. I was trying to find a job, but no one was hiring. I was getting a little concerned but holding to my faith that God would provide. My brother suggested that I go to an agency in town called West Central. They helped people out financially, and he knew people they had helped including his family. So I went there and told them my situation. They told me that they got their funding from

157

the government, and because of all the budget cuts, they were unable to help people like before, and all they could give me was twenty-five dollars. I thanked them for their time and left. Days later, someone suggested another group called the Ministerial Alliance, which had something to do with a bunch of the local churches. I contacted them, and they told them my situation, and they were also unable to help. I was totally at a loss as to what to do. I was believing in and trusting God for an answer but must admit that I was really getting concerned because I still had no job prospects. Later on, another person suggested to me another place to check for assistance called the Round-Up Program. I'd never even heard of them. The other places I had heard of but not this one. I learned of its location and went there and got an application for assistance. The lady told me to take the application home and filled it out and to have it returned with all the verification required by a certain date if I wanted to be considered for assistance. That date was about two weeks away. As I left with the application in hand, I just knew in my heart that this was a bust also. I was in need of $250, and no one had that kind of money this close to Christmas and the end of the year. With all the budget cuts and the economy down, there just wasn't any extra money out there for assistance. I had no one else to blame but myself, though. This was a bed of my own making. As I was filling out the application, I was thinking to myself that this was useless. One of the things required was a listing of all monthly expenditures. Number one for me was tithing of $100, then house payment, utilities, etc… I didn't care what they think about my tithing. It was the first thing that came out of my income right off the top before any other bill was paid. I give God what belongs to him first, then everyone else after that. I figured that alone right there would probably get my application tossed out, but I didn't care; it's the truth in my life and finances. The app also asked for proof of income and copies of things and a couple of references. After everything was filled out and all copies and proof of income were gathered, I took everything back to them and turned them in. I was told that they would be meeting in a week to make decisions on the apps they had received for assistance. I would be notified if my app was one chosen for assistance. I left that office knowing that they were not going to be able to help me either, so I decided not to look back. There was not going to be any gift exchange for Christmas this year at my house, but as long as I could fix a decent dinner for my grown daughter and me, then that's all that mattered. We would just celebrate the true meaning of Christ's birth and just be together on that day. The following week, I got a phone call from a lady for the Round-Up Program, wanting to go over my application. She said the meeting was the next night and just wanted to go over some things on my app beforehand. She asked me how I got behind on my house payment to begin with. I explained to her how it happened and that I truly believed that I would have had a job by now and made it back up. Then she asked if there was any other information I could give her that was not on my app. I told her no, that she had everything there. She then told me that I could call on Thursday afternoon to find out if my app was one that was approved for assistance. After our conversation ended, and I hung up the phone, I knew that they were not going to choose my app; it's just a feeling I had, but I thought that would be okay. I was at peace with it. Well, Thursday afternoon arrived, and I called them just so I could get the confirmation of rejection that I knew was coming. I told the lady who I was and that I was checking on my app to the Round-Up Program. She put me on hold, and a few moments later, a lady came back on and told me that, yes, my app was one of the apps that was approved for assistance by the board members. She went on to tell me that my app had been approved for $500 plus. I then replied, "Whoa! You've made a mistake. I only need $250 something." She then told me that it's no mistake, that I'd been approved for the $500-plus amount. Again, I argued with her and told her that I did not need that much money, that I only needed the $250 something. She stopped me and said, "Ms. Taylor, we approved $500 plus because we are going to make two payments for you. We are paying your January payment also." Then she said to me, "Merry Christmas, Ms. Taylor, Merry Christmas." I then burst into tears. I just couldn't believe what just happened. If that wasn't a God thing, then I don't know what is. I just knew I was going to be turned down, and I was okay with it because I *trust* in God completely. I couldn't thank her enough for what they did for me. I told her that one day when I could, I would definitely "pay it forward." I thanked her again and hung up the phone. I continued to cry happy and a little shocked tears and thanked and praised God for this. I knew without a doubt that was of God. I was truly getting to know a God I never knew before. I found myself constantly *praising God* daily for everything.

A few days later, my best friend sent me a check for $1,000 and told me to go out and get some Christmas gifts for my daughter and myself, whatever we wanted, and all the food to make an awesome Christmas dinner for her and me. More tears followed and still more praises to God. A few more days after that, I got a phone call from Wal-Mart. They asked me to come in for an interview. After the interview, I got hired on the spot, and am now employed by Wal-Mart. All of this occurred during a two-week span and at the last possible moment because I stood firm in my faith in the Lord. No one, and I mean no one, would ever convince me that God didn't have a hand in all of this. Since I gave my life back to the Lord and learned to literally trust in him alone, I'd never lacked or wanted for anything. God is good *all* the time… and *all* the time God is good. That's a phrase a dear friend Barbara Lawrence from church uses, and I have adopted that phrase for myself.

I am so very glad my dad planted the *seed* about God deep and hard in us kids when we were young. I have now returned to my faith and am learning more than I could ever have realized about a God I *never* knew growing up. I've truly learned forgiveness, especially toward Dad's wife, Betty. For the first time in my life, I felt love toward her and even told her that I love her. I *never* thought in a million years that those feelings and words would ever come from me toward her. God could change anyone's heart if you just give him the chance; I am living proof of that. I have even forgiven Rick, and we became friends again before his death. To all the others whom I felt had wronged me somewhere in my life, *I forgive you too!* I also ask for forgiveness from anyone who feels I have wronged them. I am now living to serve our Lord Jesus Christ in whatever way I am led to do.

Give God a chance. Get to know Jesus Christ, and *he* would do things for you and take you places you've never even dreamed of. Once you get to know Jesus Christ, you'll never be the same again. Go ahead and take that challenge. I dare you! I promise you won't regret it.

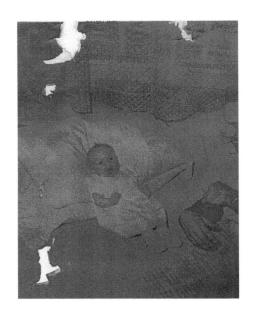

Me at about 3 or 4 months old in 1957

Me before my accident with both arms and both legs

Original newspaper article of my accident

Me in Hospital with Sister Ida and my Chatty Cathy doll

Pictures of me in hospital after accident.
Mom is reading Get well cards to me

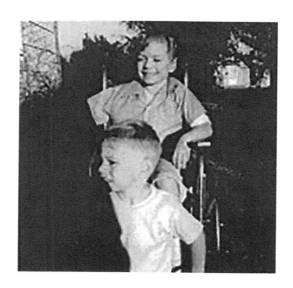

Me shortly after getting home from the
hospital with my brother Rob

Me Christmas of 1961

5 yrs old

6 yrs old

Approx 7 yrs old My Brownie Scout Uniform

8 or 9 yrs old

Age 10

Age 11

Freshman year in High School

Sophomore year in High School

Junior year in High School

Uncle Tom (dad's brother) and Aunt Betty (mom's sister)
Favorite Aunt and Uncle

Grand ma Rye and Grand dad Rye
Favorite Grandparents

My wedding day Nov 8, 1980

After wedding Reception at the Grandparents
Uncle Tom, Me, & Mom

Rick and I prior to giving birth.
I am 8 months pregnant May 1983

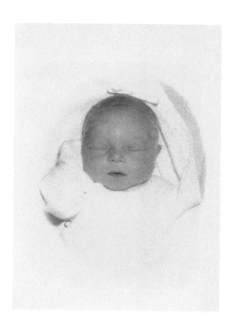

My (our) daughter Kalena Elizabeth

The only picture of my dad holding Kalena his
granddaughter at Joe's wedding. With brother David

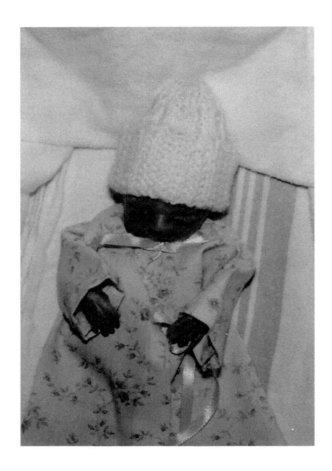

The infant girl that George and I had and lost. Kaitlyn Leanne

Visit Diana's YouTube Channel at https://www.youtube.com/user/ DianasLifeUnArmed/videos

CPSIA information can be obtained
at www.ICGtesting.com
Printed in the USA
LVHW072155121118
596925LV00011B/106/P